BECOME

The Journey of Discipleship

Copyrighted Material

ISBN: 1944166106

ISBN-13: 978-1-944166-10-6

DEDICATION

I dedicate this book to the Randolph Family. To my wife, Sharon Randolph and my children, Derrick L. Randolph Jr. and Joshua Isaiah Randolph

Table of Contents

Introduction

Welcome to Discipleship.

God is calling you to experience the Lord Jesus Christ and become like Him. It will be a demanding journey, but don't fret, you were created for this. In fact, you are commanded to do this.

It will be a wonderful journey for you, with some difficult times ahead and some rewarding moments too. You will face highs, lows and moments of rest. Wherever you find yourself, do not stress, because it's all part of the process and through it all, you will be blessed.

If you have been feeling an urge or a sense of calling to go farther in your relationship with God, then rejoice. God is giving you the opportunity to step out in faith, to become more like Jesus Christ. For it is in becoming like Jesus that we will find God's will for our lives!

Your destiny is calling.

Part I - Navigate the 5 phases of Discipleship

Follow | Reproduce | Overcome | Transform | Master

Let's begin our journey together walking through the Gospel of St. Mark. This gospel provides a unique example of Discipleship. It was written to the Gentile community about the Son of God, so they could believe and become just like Him. If you look at the life and ministry of Jesus revealed in this gospel, you can clearly see the plan for Discipleship.

"You can see the plan for Discipleship"

At age 30, Jesus began His ministry, surrendering to the will of God. He was led by the Holy Spirit to appoint ministry workers, the disciples. Then Jesus launched His ministry, experiencing the highs and lows of ministry with His workers right by His side. Jesus taught His disciples how to follow. Then He placed the ministry into their hands so they could reproduce His works. At the appointed time, they were endowed with the power of Jesus. Then they realized they were operating in the authority of Jesus. This new level of ministry, forced them to stand up to both internal and external pressures. They overcame opposition on all sides. This discipleship journey transformed them. In their thinking, believing and being they were becoming like Jesus Christ.

"They were becoming like Jesus Christ"

Jesus' journey led Him to the cross on Mt. Calvary where He would die for our sins. It signaled His moment of passion. He fulfilled His purpose. For the disciples, it was the beginning of their transformation. They would soon experience an awakening, where they would live with eyes wide opened and hearts fully committed. They would have their own sense of purpose, and their own sense of passion. Each one would have to master the highs and lows, ebbs and flows of his own discipleship journey. Jesus became obedient unto death. Now it is our turn. Let's explore this journey together. Let's grow with the disciples as we BECOME like Jesus Christ.

There are scriptures to read, lessons to learn, and actions to take. We will Follow, Reproduce, Overcome, Transform, and Master our Christian discipleship, as we BECOME.

Phase 1 – FOLLOW

Introduction – What does it mean to FOLLOW?

Let's take a look at the first phase of BECOME

Your mission of discipleship begins with a season where you will follow Jesus. You can call this a season of commitment. You will find yourself sitting at the feet of Jesus listening, learning, and believing. As you watch the master, you will discover the persecution associated with being a follower of Jesus. Expect to face accusations of all kinds, both fabricated lies and exaggerated truths. You will be introduced to obstacles that are difficult to handle. Take heed. Do not be afraid or discouraged, for the Lord God is with you.

In this phase, you will see how Jesus surrendered to the will of God. Jesus modeled what it meant for us to follow. He followed His heavenly father by praying and surrendering to the Holy Spirit of God. Then Jesus called the disciples to follow Him. They would do as He did in His everyday life. When Jesus encountered others, He administered the grace of God through the power of the Holy Spirit. The disciples would learn to do the same.

Let's watch how Jesus followed the leading of His heavenly father.
Watch how the disciples followed Jesus and do likewise!

Key lessons and events in St. Mark Chapters 1-3 include:

o   The Testimony, Baptism and Preaching of Jesus (1:1-15)
o   The Disciples call to follow (1:16-20)
o   The Disciples observe Jesus' ministry (1:21-3:19)
o   Accusations and persecution of Jesus for following God (3:20-35)

A word of Encouragement

Let me encourage you by echoing the command of the Lord Jesus Christ - Follow Him. When Jesus called His first disciples, He told them to "Come, follow me and I will send you out to fish for people." (Mark 1:17) Jesus is still calling out to us today, saying follow me! The Bible is pointing us to Jesus. There are witnesses pointing us to Jesus. There are signs of the times pointing to Jesus and His second coming. From the moment that God said, "Let us make mankind in our image, in our likeness, so that they may rule over the fish in the sea and the birds in the sky, over the livestock and all the wild animals, and over all the creatures that move along the ground." (Genesis 1:26), it was apparent that our purpose was to become like the Son of God, the Lord Jesus Christ. That means we will have to follow His way of living, develop His kind of character. To do this, we will have to study Him, by reading His scripture, learning how He loves and wholeheartedly obeying His commands. In fact, it begins with His scripture. Even Jesus said, that "Heaven and earth will pass away, but my words will never pass away." (Matthew 24:35)

Here is the challenge. The world is full of well-meaning cultures, each with their own beliefs, and value systems that are crying out for you to follow them. When you embrace them, you will join their systems, learn their teachings, embrace their style, and implement their methods of advancement.

Often times, we subject ourselves to oppression and abuse, because of our desire to go to the next level and get ahead in life. The problem is that the cultural systems and programs of the world may lead to financial gain, social status, and pleasure, lack the consignment of God and cannot provide the substance needed to produce righteousness.

The world will have you follow men on their paths of destruction, but if you follow the way of the world, you will be left holding onto hope, a dream or an empty promise. Again, follow the way of Jesus. He is "I am the way and the truth and the life." Jesus told His disciples that "No one comes to the Father except through me." (John 14:6) Follow the way that Jesus took. Follow the way of the Cross.

(Week 1 – Day 2)

Read the Testimony, Baptism and Preaching of Jesus (Mark 1:1-15)

(Week 1 – Day 3)

Read the Disciples call to follow (Mark 1:16-20)

(Week 1 – Day 4)

Read the Disciples observe Jesus' ministry (Mark 1:21-3:19)

(Week 1 – Day 5)

Read Accusations and persecution of Jesus for following God (Mark 3:20-35)

Who are you FOLLOWING?

Read the story about John the Baptist

The beginning of the good news about Jesus the Messiah, the Son of God, [2] as it is written in Isaiah the prophet:

"I will send my messenger ahead of you, who will prepare your way"— [3] "a voice of one calling in the wilderness, 'Prepare the way for the Lord, make straight paths for him.'"

[4] And so John the Baptist appeared in the wilderness, preaching a baptism of repentance for the forgiveness of sins. [5] The whole Judean countryside and all the people of Jerusalem went out to him. Confessing their sins, they were baptized by him in the Jordan River. [6] John wore clothing made of camel's hair, with a leather belt around his waist, and he ate locusts and wild honey. [7] And this was his message: "After me comes the one more powerful than I, the straps of whose sandals I am not worthy to stoop down and untie. [8] I baptize you with water, but he will baptize you with the Holy Spirit." (Mark 1:1-8)

John the Baptist came to prepare the way for Jesus to enter the hearts of the people. Jesus was coming soon and the people were not ready, so John had work to do.

When Mark introduced us to Jesus, why did he start out telling us about John the Baptist? What is the point of John the Baptist's story?

_____

_____

The point is that there is good news. God has sent His son, Jesus the Messiah, the Son of God, to make salvation available to you. John the Baptist came to pave the way for us by preaching a baptism of repentance for the forgiveness of sins.

What are the benefits of this good news? When God sent His son Jesus, what was God doing for you?

_____

_____

Here are some of God's desires:

- God was making a way for you to come out of darkness
- God sent Jesus to atone (make up) for your sins
- God made a way for you to repent of your sins
- God made a way for you to receive forgiveness for your sins
- God was setting you free from the dominion of sin
- God set you free to follow Jesus and live in relationship with Him

All of this happens when you hear the good news, believe it and act on it.

Prepare to Follow

Read verses 2-5 in the (Mark 1) John the Baptist story.

How did God prepare the people of Israel to receive the good news?
Who did God send to the people and how did they respond?

_____

_____

_____

God sent John the Baptist to warn the people by telling them that they
needed to repent. The people repented of their sins (acknowledged what
they'd done wrong) and were baptized in the Jordan River. They
prepared their hearts for the good news.

Read Isaiah 40:3-5.
Note that John the Baptist was the voice crying out in the wilderness.
What happens when the condition of your heart is made ready for Jesus?

_____

_____

God is the master planner. He always prepares for everything in
advance! To prepare the way for you, God also sent his messenger, John
the Baptist, to call out in the wilderness, telling you to prepare the way
for the Lord, to make a straight path for Him, right into your heart.

God knows what we need to believe. He did not send His son
alone. He also sent a testimony in advance. He sent John the Baptist to
give you instructions. To prepare the way, to make the path straight, to
remove all obstructions, to clear away the clutter, to remove the idols, to
destroy the allegiances that hinder your discipleship.

God's Vision

God put this plan in action because He has a Vision of Glory.
Read Mark 1:8 to help you see this vision for your life.
Do you know what God wants to accomplish in your life?

John told the people that one day they will be baptized with the
Holy Spirit. It means God's Spirit will lead them through a process of
conversion, sanctification, and empowerment. Some believe that the
evidence of this baptism is seen in the speaking in tongues, as in the day
of Pentecost, when the disciples of Jesus received power to serve as his
witnesses. Today, we understand the baptism in the Holy Spirit as the
union of your spirit with the Holy Spirit so that you can enjoy
communion (spending time) with Jesus Christ. This union of your spirit
to God's spirit is like a marriage.

How is your spiritual union with God so far? Are you holding up
your end of the relationship? In a marriage, both parties must value each
other to make it work. It requires a daily commitment to keep the
communication going. It is the same way with God.

Read Psalm 5:1-7. How comforting it is to be able talk to Him?

Read Psalm 17:1-9. What are the benefits of entering His presence?

FOLLOW JESUS' Obedience

Read the story about Jesus' baptism

At that time Jesus came from Nazareth in Galilee and was baptized by John in the Jordan. [10] Just as Jesus was coming up out of the water, he saw heaven being torn open and the Spirit descending on him like a dove. [11] And a voice came from heaven: "You are my Son, whom I love; with you I am well pleased." [12] At once the Spirit sent him out into the wilderness, [13] and he was in the wilderness forty days, being tempted by Satan. He was with the wild animals, and angels attended him.

[14] After John was put in prison, Jesus went into Galilee, proclaiming the good news of God. [15] "The time has come," he said. "The kingdom of God has come near. Repent and believe the good news!" (Mark 1:9-15)

After reading the story, go back and read verse 11.
What is the point that God wants to convey to His disciples?

_____

_____

What does God want His followers to understand?

_____

_____

The Father was pleased with His son. The Father sent His son, and His son went and did what He intended to do! If we are following Jesus, learning from His example, then the lesson here is to do what pleases our heavenly father. In this story, Jesus pleased Him by getting baptized. As a child pleases his or her parent, we have to please our father through childlike spiritual obedience.

17

In what ways could we imitate Jesus' obedience and please our heavenly father?

_____

_____

We can imitate Jesus by:
- Following His instructions
- Going where He sends us
- Enduring suffering when we have to face it
- Overcoming temptation when we have to face it

As you learn to follow and obey, you will develop the habit of spending personal time with God. During your personal time, you will discover that God has a divine assignment for you to fulfill.

Read Mark 1:9. What is the first step in Jesus' divine assignment?

_____

_____

_____

After His father spoke from heaven saying that "You are my Son, whom I love; with you I am well pleased," Jesus was led to the next step in His assignment. Where was Jesus' next step? How long did He stay there and what did he have to face?

_____

_____

_____

Divine Assignment

As you discover the 1ˢᵗ steps of your divine assignment you will realize that it will not be comfortable. You will not like it. You will be a broken vessel, living in sin, transformed into a chosen vessel, for all to see and behold the glory of the Lord.

Jesus had a divine assignment. The 1ˢᵗ step of his path was cleared out by John the Baptist. John went to the Jordan and proclaimed the message and prepared the way. Jesus had to follow the path where He would be baptized by John, validated by the father and visited by the Holy Spirit.

When you are walking in obedience, you are on public display. When this happens, who is watching? Whose lives will be impacted by your actions?

_____

_____

How does it feel knowing that when you struggle, others can see it? Since you are on public display, you might as well testify publicly!

_____

_____

_____

Acceptance

Read verse 4 in the story and write down where Jesus had to do ministry. Do you think Jesus was accepted there?

_____

_____

The reality about life is that God prepares a place for us to live. We grow in front of others. We are transformed in front of others. We become disciples, so that others will see and believe.

The truth about God revealed in this text is that God does not give us private struggles and public recognition. Jesus had to surrender to public baptism. He modeled baptism for us. For us, it symbolizes public recognition of sin, redemption, forgiveness, cleansing, and renewal into a new life in Christ.

Discuss your trials and the lessons you have learned from them.

What you must know is that after baptism, Jesus was led into the wilderness, the place of temptation, troubling, and trial.

What trials have you faced? What did it teach you about yourself?

_____

_____

_____

Now reflect on your own journey.

What you must do is find your place in the journey then realize that God is with you at every stage. Where are you on the journey? Have you experienced this part of the process where you open up about your journey and then God moves you along through it?

_____

_____

_____

FOLLOW Jesus' Calling

Read the story about the disciples' calling

As Jesus walked beside the Sea of Galilee, he saw Simon and his brother Andrew casting a net into the lake, for they were fishermen. [17] "Come, follow me," Jesus said, "and I will send you out to fish for people." At once they left their nets and followed him. When he had gone a little farther, he saw James son of Zebedee and his brother John in a boat, preparing their nets. Without delay he called them, and they left their father Zebedee in the boat with the hired men and followed him. (Mark 1:16-20)

When Jesus called the disciples they had to sacrifice something.
What are some of the things they left behind to follow Jesus?
What will Jesus teach them to do and become?

_____

_____

_____

The Main Point is that the disciples left their vocations, family businesses, for a mission assignment. They chose to fish for people, baiting them with the good news, catching them with the net of salvation, winning them to Jesus Christ, for eternal life in Him.

Jesus is inviting you to follow Him on a journey, where you will find spiritual fulfillment. You will give up a part of yourself and discover a new self on the inside.
Are you willing to leave your past life behind to follow Jesus?

_____

_____

Hunger

God may call us to physically leave others, where we do not spend as much time with them anymore. We may have to leave behind habits, hobbies, careers, loved ones, for a season or even forever as we learn to follow Jesus. It can be very hard to do, because we will miss them, but the truth about life is that you will experience some measure of hurt and pain. You will suffer human sadness sometimes. That part of life is normal, but God will be with you. He will comfort you!

Let me warn you. In life, you will find things that look great, feel great, that offer comfort, but will not be enough to satisfy your soul's desire. It will not suffice. Your soul will want more. You will crave for more out of life, and my friend, only God can satisfy!

What have you tried to quench your hunger with?

_____

_____

The truth about God revealed in this text is that God gives you something that you will have to give up. When you do, God will give you more in its place. Take a moment to reflect on your life. When it comes to leaving behind things in your life to receive more from God, how are you doing? Where are you in life? What do you have that you value most or what are you enjoying most in life? What if God required you to surrender it to Him? Could you do it?

_____

_____

_____

Open Up

When Jesus calls you to follow Him, you may miss what you gave up, and you may feel the emptiness that comes with your loss, but you must understand that what you are longing for is really God. The object of your desire is the spiritual presence of God. The constant filling of your spirit with His spirit, the constant life giving relationship, ongoing friendship and communication, and the confident feeling of love that you want can only be found by experiencing God. Only God can quench your thirst. Only God can give you the listening ear that you need. Only His voice will speak peace into your soul. Only His presence will bring calm while you are in the midst of painful circumstances. You must follow the path that leads you to reoccurring encounters with God.

What are you willing to do to open yourself up to God?
Will you let God continually fill your spirit with His life each day?
What are you willing to do to show God that you are ready?

_____

_____

_____

Are you in the crowd that has been called to follow Jesus?
Are you following the path of those who made acceptable sacrifices?
Are you in the process of turning something over to God?
Are you receiving the new assignment that He has for you?

_____

_____

_____

FOLLOW JESUS' Authority

Read the Bible Story about Jesus' authority over the impure spirit.

Just then a man in their synagogue who was possessed by an impure spirit cried out, [24] "What do you want with us, Jesus of Nazareth? Have you come to destroy us? I know who you are—the Holy One of God!" "Be quiet!" said Jesus sternly. "Come out of him!" [26] The impure spirit shook the man violently and came out of him with a shriek. (Mark 1:23-26)

What did God give to Jesus alone and no one else?

_____

_____

God gave Jesus His authority. Do you see how Jesus took authority over the situation? We sense that Jesus has authority over all of creation, even the spirits. That is why He was able to tell the impure spirit to be quiet. Should Jesus have quieted the impure spirit?

The reality about life is that we will be challenged on every level. Every aspect of our authority will be tested. Our confidence, courage and commitment will be at risk. Spiritual forces will attack us. Human enemies will face off against us. Our very own hearts will fail us.

What challenges are you facing right now?
What is threatening your authority over your own life?

_____

_____

_____

Authority

God has authority over all of creation. God had authority over each of us but God shares His authority with His followers. You can operate in God's authority, when you surrender to God's will, follow His son Jesus, doing what Jesus does, the way He does it. The good news about operating in His authority is that no enemy can defeat you. No weapon formed against you will prosper. No fear of failure will overwhelm you.

Do you believe that you have authority to do what God would do? What can authority give you permission to do?

_____

_____

_____

God wants you to follow Jesus and learn that you are a victor. As you face new trials, will you believe that you will conquer evil and God will get the glory? Are you ready to operate in your authority yet? Is your authority being tested? How will you stand in the face of danger? Are you living boldly when you speak up, pray or proclaim the truth for God?

_____

_____

_____

As you begin to move in your authority, note the times and places where you will meet people that need encouragement, care and healing. Read about Jesus' healing ministry below and prepare to discuss how Jesus used His authority to care for others and restore them from disease, pain and suffering, to whole and healthy people.

Healing

Jesus began a massive healing ministry. He heals Simon's mother-in-law who was in bed with a fever. Jesus took her hand and helped her up, and at that moment her fever left her. (Mark 1:30-31) Then a man with leprosy came begging on his knees for healing. The leprosy left this man. Though the man was supposed to show himself to the priest and make sacrifices as a testimony to the power of Jesus, he went and told everyone. People continued to see Jesus. They came from everywhere. (From Mark 1:40-45)

In Capernaum, Jesus was teaching in a crowded house, when suddenly four men tore open the roof and lowered a paralyzed man so Jesus could heal him. When Jesus saw their faith, He told the paralyzed man that his "sins are forgiven." The Teachers of the law were not believers or followers of Jesus. They were upset that Jesus forgave the man's sins, so Jesus showed them His power and authority even more, by telling the man to "Get up, take your mat and go home." [12] He got up, took his mat and walked out in full view of them all. This amazed everyone and they praised God, saying, "We have never seen anything like this!" (From Mark 2:1-12)

"Another time Jesus went into the synagogue, and healed a man with a shriveled hand by telling him to "Stretch out your hand." When the man stretched out his hand, it was completely restored. (From Mark 3:1-5) There was a religious law against healing on the sacred Sabbath day (Saturday), but Jesus proved that anytime is a good time to do good things for others and to glorify God.

Are you ready to join in with Jesus and pray for, proclaim healing for others? How ready?

_____

_____

_____

Learning who I am following like Elijah

Remember that when you encounter God, you are literally going to stop, and drop everything you are doing to follow God. When that pivotal moment of experiencing God invades the space of your life, you will literally follow God, physically, mentally, emotionally and spiritually. You will follow God's spirit, follow God's path, and follow God's ways until you walk into God's likeness. You will follow until you develop a similar lifestyle. Learning to follow is a unique calling. It means you will walk away from what is near and dear to you to follow God. You will follow until your heart begins to seek after God.

Let's take a look at how the theme FOLLOW unfolds in the life of the prophet Elijah. Let's see what it means to follow.

Elisha, the follower

Scripture

⁹When they had crossed, Elijah said to Elisha, "Tell me, what can I do for you before I am taken from you?" "Let me inherit a double portion of your spirit," Elisha replied. ¹⁰"You have asked a difficult thing," Elijah said, "yet if you see me when I am taken from you, it will be yours—otherwise, it will not." ¹¹As they were walking along and talking together, suddenly a chariot of fire and horses of fire appeared and separated the two of them, and Elijah went up to heaven in a whirlwind. ¹²Elisha saw this and cried out, "My father! My father! The chariots and horsemen of Israel!" And Elisha saw him no more. Then he took hold of his garment and tore it in two. (2 Kings 2:9-12)

As Elijah was nearing the end of his journey, his understudy, Elisha, asked for a double portion of his spirit. Elijah promised it only if Elisha hung around long enough to see Elijah taken away in a chariot of fire. Elisha answered the call to be an apprentice, aligned to succeed a great prophet and leader. Elisha learned obedient service through Elijah. He developed faith in God and patience, as he waited for his time of appointment. Though God gave him gifts, and made him great, he continued to follow Elijah. Though Elisha was becoming formed and shaped in greatness, he had the wherewithal to know that Elijah was still greater. He continued to follow Elijah until the end. Still, he was bold enough to ask for an impartation of the spirit.

Challenge

Just think about it. God has made a major investment into you. God has given you spiritual gifts. God has given you character. God has a destiny for you, a purpose and a plan to bless your life while He blesses others' lives through yours. God sees your progress. He has allowed you to peek beyond the veil to get a glimpse of your future. God knows that you know what power and purpose lives in you bustling at the seams to be lived out. For now, you are in a brief season where God is aligning you to follow great leadership. You are learning and growing, believing God and overcoming your dilemmas. God is waiting for you to want what is right. As God gives you more, God wants you to want to be more spiritual.

What will it take for you to be more spiritual?

_____

_____

_____

(Week 4 – Day 4)

Double Blessing

Ask for the double blessing. Ask for the gift of the spirit, the anointing of the spirit, the relationship with God through fellowship with His spirit. When you do, expect responsibility, and the accountability that goes with it. You may have been following, but God is waiting for you to learn how to follow with integrity.

Read Job 2:2-10

When Satan was "roaming throughout the earth, the LORD asked Satan, "Have you considered my servant Job? There is no one on earth like him; he is blameless and upright, a man who fears God and shuns evil." Job maintained his integrity, even though his life was ruined without reason.

What is integrity to you and how can you demonstrate it in your Christian life?

_____

_____

_____

Now, let's pickup on the story of the prophet Elijah and learn how to keep pace. We pick up on Elijah's story after a major victory, where he faces a major threat against his life and he is hiding out, no longer trusting in God. Elijah must determine if he will get back up and follow God or fade into obscurity as a great prophet of God.

In the first book of Kings, chapter sixteen, we find Ahab, king of Israel who was doing evil in the eyes of the Lord. Ahab abandoned the LORD's commands, worshipped the false god of Baal and angered the Lord, the God of Israel. God sent Elijah the prophet into a period of consecration in the Kerith Ravine, east of the Jordan. When God was ready to confront Ahab, Elijah invited the people of Israel to Mount Carmel where they would witness Elijah contending with the 450 prophets of Baal and the 400 prophets of Asherah. They each called on the name of their god. Elijah's God answered by fire. Elijah defeated and slaughtered the false prophets. The people all fell prostrate and cried, "The LORD—he is God!

Learning that I am a successor like Elijah

Scripture

Now Ahab told Jezebel everything Elijah had done and how he had killed all the prophets with the sword. So Jezebel sent a messenger to Elijah to say, "May the gods deal with me, be it ever so severely, if by this time tomorrow I do not make your life like that of one of them." (1 Kings 19:1-2)

Elijah was not out of the clear yet. Jezebel sent a messenger to Elijah with a threat on his life. This time, "Elijah was afraid and ran for his life." (1 Kings 19:3a)

The great prophet of God, Elijah defeats the false prophets of Baal at Mt. Horeb. After such a monumental feat, his enemy retreats to go get backup, as Ahaz runs to get the assistance of Jezebel. The enemy is waiting to bring in extra resources to fight the battle. But God also has resources. God can send in people and angels. God can move supernaturally by His spirit. God uses helpers, people who will step in and serve God when needed. When the servants of God need to retreat and go to God for backup, God uses His resources. That's where you come in. You are a helper, a servant of God, a disciple that follows the Lord Jesus Christ.

God is doing great things in and through His people. God needs you to be His willing helper. We are God's servants, leaders and followers.

Challenge

Are you ready to follow? God is preparing you to succeed someone on a mission for Him. Ask yourself and pray (ask God) if you are available to be used by God at a moment's call?

Sign of Hope

God has a plan for your life. The plan is ready. The place is ready. Now, God has to get you ready. The sign of hope is that God is working on you. That's proof that He's getting everything else ready for you. Now, make yourself available to God now. Start surrendering!

FOLLOW Effectively (Memory Verse & Action Plan)
Understanding your salvation (Assurance of Salvation)

And this is the testimony: God has given us eternal life, and this life is in his Son. Whoever has the Son has life; whoever does not have the Son of God does not have life. (1 John 5:11-12)

Read Genesis 22:1-19 about Abraham's Sacrifice. It is a foretelling of God's salvation.
1. God told Abraham to offer his son _____as a _____
2. Isaac said here is the fire and the wood: but where is the lamb for a burnt offering? Abraham said, God will provide himself a _____ for a burnt offering
3. When Abraham took the knife, the angel of the LORD said…"for now I know that you _____ God, since you have not withheld your only son from me."
4. I will bless you and multiply your _____ as numerous as the stars in heaven

Answers - (Isaac, burnt offering, lamb, fear, seed)

Read and discuss Matthew 27:27-56 Jesus' Crucifixion
The soldiers mocked and humiliated Jesus Identify ways the soldiers mocked & humiliated Jesus.
- The soldiers stripped Jesus
- They put a scarlet robe on him
- They twisted together a crown of thorns and put it on his head
- They put a staff in his right hand.
- They knelt in front of him and mocked him.
- They said, "Hail, king of the Jews!"
- They spit on him
- They took the staff and struck him on the head again and again.
- They led him away to crucify him.

Now Get Prepared. Get Ready!

God is doing something big! God is using someone to do it. At some point, God will move you in to succeed that person. You will do that work. You will assume a great responsibility. You are worried about what you are called to do, what your purpose is, what you will do to make a difference. God already knows the plans he has for you. God knows what is on your plate. You are not ready for it today, not right now, but your time will come.

God has to begin preparing you little by little. He has small assignments for you to work on. You will learn to trust Him a little at a time. You will develop a little faith now, the size of a mustard seed. You will develop greater faith as you go each day, to move mountains, to speak a word of encouragement, to minister to broken souls, to lead persons to Christ. To use the gifts of the spirit imparted into you. You don't know what God has for you. Only God knows. He will develop the faith in you, mature the spirit in you, and align you and the nuances of your life so you are in a the proper position and posture to hear from God, know God's voice, trust God's plans even when you don't understand. God will prepare you to be able to handle heavy weight assignments. It will come to past before you realize it is here.

Your time is near. God will use someone else on an assignment and when they are no longer needed, God will move you in. Get prepared by God, in God and for God now! For now learn to follow. One day you will lead. Throughout the journey you will BECOME!

FOLLOW ACTION PLAN

Review this chapter's lessons and list your FOLLOW Goals.
These are your next steps to help you BECOME.

Here are some examples:

- Thank God Daily for providing for you. He wants to surprise you in your time of need
- Recognize God's strength and acknowledge that He has all power
- Be attentive to His spirit so you can sense when He wants to visit you and spend time with you.
- Spend time in prayer and in listening so that He can hear, learn and understand His voice.
- Meditate on the word each day, opening your spirit to God so He can reveal Himself to you.
- Pray to understand God, so that you will know who is working behind the scenes (in the spirit) making things line up for you)
- Remind yourself each morning that God will make you victorious in everything you do for Him
- Let your understanding of God grow slowly over time.

_____

_____

_____

_____

_____

_____

FOLLOW ACKNOWLEDGMENT

Read and sign your personal 'Agreement to become"

Ask your Discipleship Leader to sign and agree

I acknowledge that I will walk in reverence of God. I agree to treat God's name with admiration and honor, having full confidence in Him as he provides my needs and blesses my life.

_____

Disciple

I accept the responsibility to hold this disciple accountable by making sure he/she walks in humble submission and service to the Lord.

_____

Discipleship Leader

Phase 2 - REPRODUCE

Introduction to REPRODUCE

First you learn to follow. Then you learn to reproduce. You will have to watch and learn, copy and paste, show and tell what you've learned. In our churches there are elders, leaders, and others who have poured into us. Now they wish to see our progress. Now, it is time to demonstrate your faith. It's time to walk in the power and authority that has been shared with you. God delegated it to you. He invested it in to you. You will have to demonstrate the power that you witnessed and experienced for yourself. By grace through face, you have received salvation. Now you will exercise power over demons.

Not only will you exercise the power and reveal the authority given to you, you will also walk in it together with other disciples. In some cases you will speak up for others. You will even suffer for it. Eventually, you will exercise faith for the benefit of others, helping others have faith as well. In this phase, Jesus taught the disciples a few principles of faith. Jesus explained how to exercise power and authority, how to have faith for others, and how to help others have faith.

Key lessons and events in **Mark Chapters 4-7** include:

o   Jesus' teaching on sowing, reaping and having faith (4:1-34)
o   Jesus' demonstration of power, authority (4:35-41)
o   Jesus' demonstration of power over demons, death (5:1-6:6)
o   Disciples sent out together (6:7-6:13)
o   John speaking up and suffering (6:14-29)
o   Jesus' demonstration of faith for others (6:30-56)
o   Jesus' helping others have faith (Ch. 7)

One of the most satisfying things in life is to develop a routine that you follow each day. When you learn your routine there's no feeling like it. It is an awesome experience when you are getting into the flow, not thinking about what you are doing, but doing it.

Right when you find your flow in life, the Lord Jesus Christ finds a way to break in and crash in on your routine. What He does is show you His routine, how He lives each day. He is fully God fully man, living in the natural world but also living in the spirit world. It is beautiful! He came to minister to spirits, calling us to repentance, offering us forgiveness and then ministering to us. Jesus' routine involved His loving, preaching, teaching and healing. Jesus came to deliver and restore us into fellowship with Him. These are the works of God.

Jesus did many things that we were blessed to see, understand and experience in the natural world. He also did many miracles for us to experience in the Spirit. Remember we are spirits living in a spiritual world, and humans living in the natural world of flesh and blood. Jesus' ministry involved both our human body and our spirits.

Now for us disciples, Jesus taught us how to follow Him, imitating Him and replicate His words. Jesus walked and talked and ate food and lived among people, but He ministered to their spirits. That's something that no one else could do. Jesus taught His disciples how to do it too. I encourage you to do likewise. See people in the flesh, but also see them in the spirit and minister to them in the spirit.

Go live among people and faithfully replicate the works of God. Operate in the authority of God. Demonstrate the power of God. Let no demon of fear or death stop you. Speak up for what is right. Speak truth with love. Even those in power will have to surrender and respond. They will test your spirit for love. They will test your words against the Word. They will determine if their power should yield to your God. Be steadfast and immoveable if Jesus sent you.

Week 5 - Day 2
Read Jesus' teaching on sowing, reaping and having faith (4:1-34)

Week 5 - Day 3
Read Jesus' demonstration of power, authority (4:35-41)
Read Jesus' demonstration of power over demons, death (5:1-6:6)

Week 5 - Day 4
Read Disciples sent out together (6:7-6:13)
Read John speaking up and suffering (6:14-29)
Read Jesus' demonstration of faith for others (6:30-56)

Week 5 - Day 5
Read Jesus' helping others have faith (Ch. 7)

What are you REPRODUCING?

One evening when Jesus and His disciples were on a boat, a storm with heavy waves swamped the boat. Since Jesus was still sleep during the storm, the disciples woke him and asked, "Teacher, don't you care if we drown?" [39] He got up, rebuked the wind and said to the waves, "Quiet! Be still!" Then the wind died down and it was completely calm. [40] He said to his disciples, "Why are you so afraid? Do you still have no faith?" (From Mark 4:35-40)

Calm in the midst of the storm

In life you can choose to become like Jesus and walk through life in faith or you can continue to live the way the world teaches you to and react to life in fear.

Whose work will you reproduce?

How are you when troubles come? Are you calm or chaotic? Do you get rowdy and out of sorts or do you settle down and get focused on the one who is greater than the storm?

_____

_____

_____

Read Isaiah 43:2 and discuss the promises that God has for you.

_____

_____

God's presence is enough. Now that you know that God is with you, you must understand that God wants you to calm down when trouble comes. He will help you calm yourselves, your fears and emotions. God does not want us filled with anxiety. He wants us to have confident faith in Him. When the situations we are in are like storms swirling around us, charging at us like waves, trying to drown us with worry and doubt, we have to remain calm and trust that God can calm the storm.

Read another promise from the prophet Isaiah in Isaiah 54:17 and discuss how God protects you.

_____

_____

We should never be afraid of the storms of life!

After Jesus taught the disciples how to calm the storm (and calm themselves) down, He showed them how to deliver someone from a demon. When Jesus, the Son of the Most High God, went across the lake to the region of the Gerasenes, He encountered a man with an impure spirit who lived in the tombs. Once again Jesus went where no man would go (in the tombs) and did what no other would do (deliver the man from the impure spirit). Jesus showed that He had the kind of power that no one else had. 'He has authority over all of creation.'

Tolerance for the tormented

Read Mark 5:1-8 and discuss your willingness to minister to the demon possessed.

Are you prepared to minister to people who are under the control of impure spirits? Some persons live in chaos, unhinged, with no rules, nor restraint. They are suffering because their impulses drive them out of control? Someday they will hear about the healing power of Jesus Christ. Until they are able to develop their own personal relationship with God, they will seek refuge in disciples who follow Jesus and walk in His power.

How will you respond when someone under the power of Legion approaches you?

_____

_____

_____

Later, Jesus went to heal the dying daughter of Jairus, one of the synagogue leaders. Jesus put everyone out, he took the child's father and mother and the disciples with him, and went in where the child was. [41] He took her by the hand and said to her, *"Talitha koum!"* (which means "Little girl, I say to you, get up!"). (Mark 5:40-41).

Jesus wanted the disciples to have faith in all situations. Even when others have no hope, His disciples should have faith and do the impossible. Even when others are afraid (e.g. of sickness and death), Jesus wants His disciples to see the limitless possibilities that only God can provide. Jesus wants His disciples to go, care, heal and deliver His people from their diseases.

After the young girl encountered Jesus, she stood up and began to walk around. Jesus only brought a few witnesses with Him to watch the miracle take place. Are you one of His witnesses? Do you believe that Jesus can do anything? Are you a witness to the miraculous power of God? What has your faith in Jesus allowed you to see so far?

_____

_____

_____

Have faith now in what Jesus will do for others later. Put your faith in Jesus now. Then go and believe God for the same miracles to take place before your very eyes.

When Jesus was on His way to Jairus' house to heal his daughter, Jesus was stopped by a woman who was sick and had spent all of her money on doctors but only became worse. When she heard about Jesus, she found him surrounded by a crowd. She came up behind him and touched his cloak, because she thought, "If I just touch his clothes, I will be healed." When Jesus realized that she accessed His power, He told her, "Daughter, your faith has healed you. Go in peace and be freed from your suffering." He wanted onlookers to have faith like this woman, to access His power like this woman, to become humble like this woman, to enter the presence of God because He is available.

When Jesus healed the woman who had been sick for 12 years, the first spiritual lesson worth noting is that when our very survival is at stake, we can overcome all odds by faith. When the woman touched Jesus' cloak, the disciples needed to bear witness to someone else's great act of faith. Not only do we need to do the great works that Jesus Himself did, we should also acknowledge and validate faith in others when it is at work.

Read Mark 5:25-34 and list everything that happened as a result of her faith.

_____

_____

_____

_____

Now list everything in your life that you would like to change as a result of your faith.

_____

_____

_____

_____

Close this section out with a prayer of faith in the name of Jesus!

Have you ever wondered how much healing takes place in God's presence? What areas of our lives will be healed when we enter the presence of the Lord?

_____

_____

_____

Healing

Is there anyone in your life that you believe needs healing?

Take a moment to pray for their healing. Write it out.

_____

_____

_____

_____

_____

God told the prophet Habakkuk (Habakkuk 2:2) to "write down the revelation and make it plain on tablets." Today we say, write the vision and make it plain.

For this exercise, it means, write down what you believe it will look like when that person is healed. Then celebrate what God is going to do.

_____

_____

_____

_____

Read the testimony of Jesus Christ in Isaiah 53:1-5 and rest assured that God has healing for available for us all.

According to this scripture, why are you healed already?

_____

_____

_____

_____

Always be prepared to believe and pray for other's healing.

Write a prayer of healing today for the souls that you will encounter on your discipleship journey that will need healing?

_____

_____

_____

_____

_____

REPRODUCE by Feeding the Crowd

When Jesus landed and saw a large crowd, he had compassion on them, because they were like sheep without a shepherd. So he began teaching them many things. [35] By this time it was late in the day, so his disciples came to him. "This is a remote place," they said, "and it's already very late. [36] Send the people away so that they can go to the surrounding countryside and villages and buy themselves something to eat." [37] But he answered, "You give them something to eat." They said to him, "That would take more than half a year's wages[a]! Are we to go and spend that much on bread and give it to them to eat?" [38] "How many loaves do you have?" he asked. "Go and see." When they found out, they said, "Five—and two fish." [39] Then Jesus directed them to have all the people sit down in groups on the green grass. [40] So they sat down in groups of hundreds and fifties. [41] Taking the five loaves and the two fish and looking up to heaven, he gave thanks and broke the loaves. Then he gave them to his disciples to distribute to the people. He also divided the two fish among them all. [42] They all ate and were satisfied, [43] and the disciples picked up twelve basketfuls of broken pieces of bread and fish.[44] (Mark 6:34-45)

Have you ever noticed how easily God provides for us when we simply trust Him? God provided a young boy who had 5 loaves of bread and 2 fish. Then God fed 5000 people who were hungry.

What are the most common needs that people have today?

_____

_____

_____

What would happen if you had a little faith and someone brought you a little help (like the little boy)?

_____

_____

_____

Read Isaiah 41:8-10 and list God's promises to help His servants

When you see others in need, use your faith to pray for them. As you care for others, and move the heart of God, be prepared to watch God provide for others. Be prepared to be God's hands, serving others.

_____

_____

_____

Walk on the Water

Later after feeding 5000, Jesus was on land when He saw the disciples trapped on their boat in the middle of the storm. Jesus walked on water and went out to meet them. Jesus may have been trying to teach them that God can do anything, that by faith, they can overcome anything, even by walking on water. They can overcome the storms. They can should have realized that God will provide all of their needs.

When they saw him, they thought he was a ghost, but Jesus said, "Take courage! It is I. Don't be afraid."

Read Mark 6:47-56. List 2 ways they believed Jesus would heal them.

_____

_____

What are some of the sicknesses, worries or fears that you have, that mere faith in Jesus will help you overcome?

_____

_____

_____

_____

Trust God. Nothing can separate you from the Love of God.

Read Revelation 12:11 and list the 2 weapons that Jesus' witnesses will use to triumph over the enemy (the devil) in the last days.

_____

_____

Use your weapons. Take comfort in knowing that you have them today. The blood of Jesus gives us power and the word of our testimony (in Jesus) has power. They help us to stand in the face of danger. They help us to remain faithful when we face trials. They remind us that we can do all things through Christ who gives us strength. Plead the blood of Jesus in the time of trouble. The blood of Jesus will work on your behalf.

How to REPRODUCE (Lessons from Elijah)

Let's take a look at how the theme reproduce unfolds in the life of the prophet Elijah. Let's look at what it means to reproduce

Learn to obey like Elijah

Scripture - Then he lay down under the bush and fell asleep. All at once an angel touched him and said, "Get up and eat." He looked around, and there by his head was some bread baked over hot coals, and a jar of water. He ate and drank and then lay down again. (1 Kings 19:5-6)

Think About It!

God Strengthened Elijah.

God commanded Elijah to get up. He provided for Elijah, and strengthened Elijah with food that was waiting for Elijah.

Thanks be to God! What Elijah needed was already there. Elijah only had to obey God to receive it.

Elijah ate just enough to gain his strength, and he laid back down! (Lol)

He needed food for strength. He needed strength to rest and rest for the journey.

Like Elijah, we need food, strength and rest too! We get tired and too weak to stand spiritually. Remember, God gives us everything we need.

Challenge

What do you need today? Do you need spiritual food to build you up? Do you need spiritual strength to help you fight? Do you need spiritual rest from a battle you've just won?

Sign of Hope

Just obey God. You don't know what you need. God knows. Just obey and everything will be waiting for you.

Learn to serve God first like Elijah

Scripture

The angel of the LORD came back a second time and touched him and said, "Get up and eat, for the journey is too much for you." So he got up and ate and drank. Strengthened by that food, he traveled forty days and forty nights until he reached Horeb, the mountain of God. (1 Kings 19:7-8)

Think About It!

Elijah went on yet another journey

Some want to give direction. Some want to lead and some want to follow, but everyone must learn to follow God's directions

Challenge

Sometimes you think you are ready but you aren't quite ready for the next assignment yet. What test, trial or lesson are you learning for a 2nd time in life? What are you struggling with that God is requiring you to endure? It may be that God wants you fully prepared to conquer it in this next season of your life.

Sign of Hope

Having to do something again means that you get to learn deeper lessons this time around. Just endure it! Learn to obey God regardless of where you are in life and you will have joy when you finish. God's got you and He knows exactly what you need for success.

Elisha, the reproducer

Scripture

Elisha then picked up Elijah's cloak that had fallen from him and went back and stood on the bank of the Jordan. He took the cloak that had fallen from Elijah and struck the water with it. "Where now is the LORD, the God of Elijah?" he asked. When he struck the water, it divided to the right and to the left, and he crossed over. (2 Kings 2:13-14)

Think about It!

When Elijah left in the chariot of fire, Elijah's cloak fell to him. He immediately tested to see if he could pick up where Elijah left off in his relationship with God. He struck the water with the cloak and divided the waters of the Jordan. Elisha walked across the Jordan on dry ground. He received confirmation that the type of relationship that Elijah had, he too would have. The faith in God that Elijah had, he too would have. Access to God, he too would have; miracles, he too would have. Yes, Elisha asked "where now is the Lord, the God of Elijah". Well, the Lord, the God of Elijah showed up and demonstrated His power. Elisha has been empowered to reproduce the works of Elijah. He will be able to serve and obey God. Elijah parted the waters and crossed the Jordan on dry ground. This was symbolic of his crossing from follower to reproducer. Elisha would soon be transformed into an even greater disciple and leader.

Challenge

Are you waiting for someone to give you permission to do greater works? Jesus has equipped you. What do you need from God to get you started?

Sign of Hope

You too, will come face to face with your destiny in your moment of reckoning. You will have to reproduce the works that you've been exposed to.

REPRODUCE Effectively (Memory Verse & Action Plan)

Assurance of Trust – Proverbs 3:5-6

Trust in the LORD with all your heart and lean not on your own understanding; in all your ways submit to him, and he will make your paths straight.

We have an "Assurance" (i.e. promise, guarantee) that trusting God works. Trusting God is relying on God and having confidence in Him.

- The Bible teaches us to rely on God and on the character of God, especially for the promises God makes to us in the Bible.
- Trust is the belief that someone or something is reliable, good, honest, effective, etc. Trust is dependence on something future or reliance on future payment for property (as merchandise)
- It is an arrangement in which someone's property or money is legally held or managed by someone else or by an organization (such as a bank) for usually a set period of time
- It is reliance on the character, ability, strength, or truth of someone or something

You are trusting in God when you have confidence in God, when you are relying on God for today and depending on God for your future.

God wants us to trust God for eternal salvation and rescue from today's circumstances.

Some **trust** in chariots and some in horses, but we trust in the name of the Lord our God. (Psalm 20:7)

ACTION PLAN

Review this chapter's lessons and list your REPRODUCE Goals.
These are your next steps to help you BECOME

Here are some examples:

- Take authority in the realm of the spirit
- Pray to God in your heavenly language
- Speak to people in a way that they can understand the gospel
- Lay hands on the sick and watch them get well

_____

_____

_____

_____

_____

_____

_____

_____

REPRODUCE ACKNOWLEDGMENT

Read and sign your personal 'Agreement to become"

Ask your Discipleship Leader to sign and agree

I acknowledge that I will walk in God's authority, command God's power to do God's will, in the season that I am in. I will stand up, speak up, rise up, and show up to the fight whenever God wants me to reproduce His works among men.

_____

Disciple

I accept the responsibility to hold this disciple accountable by making sure he/she walks in humble submission and service to the Lord.

_____

Discipleship Leader

Phase 3 - OVERCOME

Introduction to OVERCOME

A season of following (learning) leads to imitating (doing it yourself). The more you walk in the faith, the more you will face your own hardships. The master (Jesus) faced hardships. Some of them were not revealed to us but scripture shows enough of the opposition Jesus faced for us to see that it was not an easy walk for the Lord. Like the master, you too will have to overcome opposition.

Jesus and the disciples faced tremendous opposition from the Pharisees. There was opposition from unbelievers. The disciples opposed themselves as they struggled with doubt, feelings of shame for following Jesus and the unwillingness to suffer for following Jesus. Jesus gave them opportunity to identify with Him, and overcome their foes of opposition.

Key lessons and events in Mark Chapter 8 include:

o   Opposition from unbelievers (Pharisees) (8:1-21)
o   The opposition of brokenness (8:22-25)
o   The opposition of doubt (8:26-30)
o   The opposition to suffering (8:31-33)
o   The opposition of shame (8:34-38)

A word of Encouragement

We are all people with problems. We have our own fears. We are at times timid and afraid. We are at times overconfident and overzealous. We are wired to fail. It is so hard to overcome our own limitations but we have to overcome them.

Jesus does not want us to look at ourselves too long because if we do we will see our limitations and flaws. We will lose faith, feel incapable of following Jesus, doing what He did and continuing on the journey. Jesus does not want us to look at others either; for, we will see their faces, their discouragement, and their lack of faith in God. Then we will transpose those things on to ourselves and fail to believe that we can do the works of God. No, the Lord wants us to look to Him; for Peter looked to Jesus and walked on water. Then he looked at the water, and waves and started to fail. Behold, the Lamb of God when we look to Him we believe we can do all things. We have to overcome all of the doubts and fears and wearisome discouragement in the world

The good news is that we don't have to overcome them all one by one. We simply have to look to Jesus to let go of the world. Set aside some time. Activate our faith in the Lord Jesus and follow Him. Then we'll overcome everything else. We will reach our destination if we stop looking at what we're afraid of, stop looking at ourselves for strength and only look to Jesus, it will require all of your faith. You can and will overcome!

Week 9 – Day 2

Read Opposition from unbelievers (Pharisees) (8:1-21)

Week 9 – Day 3
Read the opposition of brokenness (8:22-25)
Read the opposition of doubt (8:26-30)

Week 9 – Day 4
Read the opposition to suffering (8:31-33)

Week 9 – Day 5
Read the opposition of shame (8:34-38)

How are you OVERCOMING?

Read the story about the miraculous feeding of 4000.
Jesus miraculously fed 4000 with 7 loaves of bread and a few small fish.
Here, Jesus performs another miracle to help the unbelieving generation
see and believe. It would better if they simply had faith that God sent His
one and only son. Unfortunately, not everyone believed. The Pharisees
went to Jesus and asked for a sign from heaven. Jesus told them that He
would not give them a sign.

Read Mark 8:6-15. Discuss some reasons people pray to God for a sign.

_____

_____

_____

      In some cases, we want a sign from God to affirm the desires we
privately and selfishly have hidden in our hearts. Other times we want a
sign because we do not believe what God has already provided.
Jesus was the sign that men were looking for. He was the sign of God's
love. He was the sign that would point me to God's salvation. Jesus was
the sign of redemption. God had already sent His son as a sign to a
wicked and adulterous generation that would not believe God.

The problem with the Pharisees is that they were the leaders of a generation of people that were living in a state of sin, separated from the presence of God. The Pharisees were enjoying the luxuries and benefits of being the religious leaders, but they were not fulfilling their religious responsibilities. They did not know God for themselves either. So, when God sent His son, Jesus Christ as a sign of His loving kindness and Jesus preached that everyone should repent of their sins, the Pharisees did not want to accept that Jesus' coming was really God at work. They were too ashamed to admit that they were hiding behind their own sin.

REFLECTION - Take a moment to pause and reflect.

Do you have any unconfessed sin in your own life? Is there any part of you that feels empty, alone, broken? Can you admit that you need more of God's presence in your life? Take this time to acknowledge it (in prayer). Ask God to heal your broken places, strengthen you where you are weak and to fill you with His presence. Spend time (now) thanking God for answering your prayers.

Your Testimony

There is an Old Testament story about the prophet Jonah who was sent by God to the town of Nineveh to protest against its wickedness. Jonah felt that the Ninevites were evil toward his people (Hebrews), so he rebelled against God and took **a** ship in the opposite direction. A storm arose, and the sailors eventually threw Jonah overboard where he was swallowed by a great fish (whale) until he repented (3 days later). Eventually Jonah preached to the Ninevites and they repented of their evil ways.

The story teaches us that after 3 days of living in the belly of a whale, Jonah repented of his sin and turned in the right direction (to obey God). The Ninevites repented as well. Jesus was telling the Pharisees that if the Ninevites could repent of their sin, then the Pharisees could too. The Ninevites will stand before God one day as a witness and as a sign to this generation that they should have repented too. Jesus knew that He was going to die on the cross and spend 3 days in hell (similar to Jonah) and that is all the sign that people need.

Read Matthew 12:38-41 about the sign of Jonah.

Think about what your testimony will be to the world when you stand before God. What will they say about your life? Did you turn your life around? Did you become a true disciple of Jesus Christ? When the unbelieving world stands in judgment before the throne of God, what will they remember about your life? Was it a sign that God was doing something?

_____

_____

_____

_____

_____

When people look at your life, they should see the outward glow of a person that is experiencing God. God's word and God's spirit are at work in and through you!

Jesus wanted the Pharisees and others to admit to themselves that God was at work in their lives. As disciples, you will face opposition from others. You will have to stand up to others and declare that Jesus Christ is the Son of God, sent from heaven to redeem mankind from their state of sin.

Promises

Read God's promise to the Hebrew children in Exodus 23:20-30.

They were following God's angel to inherit their Promised Land.

What are the ways that God promised to defend His people?

_____

_____

_____

What will God do to those who oppose you?

_____

_____

_____

OVERCOME Poor self-perception

Read the Bible Story

They came to Bethsaida, and some people brought a blind man and begged Jesus to touch him. [23] He took the blind man by the hand and led him outside the village. When he had spit on the man's eyes and put his hands on him, Jesus asked, "Do you see anything?" [24] He looked up and said, "I see people; they look like trees walking around." [25] Once more Jesus put his hands on the man's eyes. Then his eyes were opened, his sight was restored, and he saw everything clearly. [26] Jesus sent him home, saying, "Don't even go into the village." (Mark 8:22-26)

This is an unusual miracle about a man who was born blind. It is unusual because Jesus spit on the man's eyes. He did not simply touch his eyes. Nor did Jesus put mud on them. He spit on the man's eyes and touched them, but the man was not fully healed and restored. This was a first. When Jesus asked him, "Do you see anything?" the man looked up and said, "I see people; they look like trees walking around."

This man was faced with the opposition of poor self-perception. Jesus' touched him twice. After the 2nd touch, "his eyes were opened, his sight was restored, and he saw everything clearly." Perhaps the first touch had to work on his mind, or his own self-image. Maybe he had been feeling so low, since he was a blind beggar. His status was low in society. His image of others was so great, since he saw them as great as trees walking around. Maybe his soul was broken, fractured from the feeling of abandonment from the world. He may have needed to see with a strengthened heart and mind working as one. Whatever the cause, it took a second touch and after the second touch, the blind man could see clearly and live whole.

Has God ever given you a second touch? Have you ever had a poor self-perception that it took time to repair? Has God ever had to lower your admiration for others? Has God taught you to lift Him up higher, so that you have greater reverence for Him? Write about it!

_____

_____

_____

_____

_____

_____

_____

_____

Discuss how God balances your perception of yourself, others and God.

In the story about the blind man who received his sight, we have to remember that he lived his life in a state of sin. He lived a broken life of suffering, low self-esteem, and disconnection from his God, his community and within himself. God is always reaching out to those who will turn from a life of sin to a life of loving obedience to God.

Read Psalm 34:4-9
What are the promises of God for those who seek and fear the Lord?

_____

_____

_____

When the blind man was restored, Jesus told him "Don't even go into the village." The village (your community) is sometimes a nursery for hope. The village, a place the nurtures you, builds you up and prepares you to go out and do great things. On the contrary, your village (community) may be a place of sin that harbors unbelief, and God may desire that you leave it for a season, to reflect on God, to think about what He has done for you, and to grow in the knowledge and understanding of Jesus Christ. Sometimes God sends you away from the crowds, so you can see spiritually and believe for yourself.

The disciples did not understand the significance of Jesus feeding the 5000 or the 4000 or the healing of the blind man. They had not spent time reflecting on what God had done. As disciples, we have to overcome the opposition of blindness. The disciples were spiritually blind. The man who was just healed suffered various forms of blindness (physical, spiritual, social).

This was evident later when Jesus taught that He must suffer rejection, death and resurrection. His disciple, Peter argued with Jesus about it, but Jesus replied, "Get behind me, Satan! You do not have in mind the concerns of God, but merely human concerns." (Mark 8:33)

Our lesson from this is that we disciples have to overcome our allegiance to the way the world sees things. If we are going to reproduce the faith and the works of Jesus, then we have to develop our allegiance to Jesus Christ. We must think about the things that concern God. Then we will see things the way Jesus sees them. He is Lord and King in the spiritual world. In the spirit, He reigns and He alone gives us sight to follow Him and to do what He does and to see the forces of opposition that we need to overcome.

Discuss the works of God that you are able to see spiritually (today) that you could not see before.

_____

_____

_____

_____

_____

OVERCOME the opposition of shame

Read the Bible Story

Then he called the crowd to him along with his disciples and said: "Whoever wants to be my disciple must deny themselves and take up their cross and follow me. [35] For whoever wants to save their life will lose it, but whoever loses their life for me and for the gospel will save it. [36] What good is it for someone to gain the whole world, yet forfeit their soul? [37] Or what can anyone give in exchange for their soul? [38] If anyone is ashamed of me and my words in this adulterous and sinful generation, the Son of Man will be ashamed of them when he comes in his Father's glory with the holy angels." (Mark 8:34-38)

Do you really want to be a disciple of Jesus Christ?

_____

The name Jesus is synonymous with the cross that Jesus would have to bear. It was considered a capital punishment by the Romans and retaliation by the Jewish leaders. God planned it to atone for the sins of all humanity. For Jesus, it would be a sacrifice that cost Him his life.

When you decide to follow Jesus, you are agreeing to deny yourself. In every generation, the elders would agree that we generally do not deny ourselves much 'these days'. Nevertheless, if you will become a disciple of Jesus Christ, you are agreeing to submit yourself to the standards that Jesus set. To meet the standards, you have to agree to the principles and teachings of Jesus. Then as you try to do the works of Jesus, you have to agree to the rigor required to get up to par.

Circle every example of denying yourself

Relying on my feelings alone (when responding to criticism)
Making my decisions alone (without praying to God)
Spending time in prayer when I would rather watch TV

Mark each statement as T/F

o   Taking up your cross is the same as sacrificing your life for Jesus since He sacrificed His life for you.

o   Taking up your cross means you have to literally die like Jesus died

o   Taking up your cross means you are making a daily sacrifice the same way Jesus did

If you really want to become a disciple, Jesus requires that you take a long hard look at the life that you have been living on your own and for yourself. Jesus wants you to stop and consider if you are able to sacrifice your life for Jesus and His gospel. It is easy to agree to it, and to begin the journey, but at some point, you may look back at what you have been missing out on and then decide to lay down your cross and go pick your old life back up. Imagine that! Jesus knows that some of us may look at how much suffering is required to be a disciple and then walk away.

Decide today to receive His spirit and preserve your soul!
Decide today to walk with Jesus in obedience to the word of God.

As you do, one of the challenges that you will face is that you will encounter opponents of Jesus Christ who will threaten your life if you stand for Jesus and the gospel. I encourage you today to decide right now that you will not be ashamed. Be proud of Jesus and His words of life.

Even if you stand alone, for a long time, when no one else will stand with you, you must overcome the fear of shame and guilt that the enemies of God want you to feel.

Read Genesis (6:11-13, 17-22) and discuss how Noah must have felt being the only person that had heard and received instructions from God. Imagine building a boat to protect you and your family (alone) from a flood that no one else knew about.

Think about it. Could your friends, family or neighbors convince you to quit building the arc because it seemed ridiculous? Would you have grown tired of building it and have returned to your old life? Would you have felt stupid in front of people that you can see once you had received instructions from a God that no one could see? Write about it!

_____

_____

_____

_____

_____

_____

In a letter that the Apostle Paul wrote to the churches in Rome, he declared "For I am not ashamed of the gospel, because it is the power of God that brings salvation to everyone who believes." (Romans 1:16a)

In closing list some of the ways that the gospel helps people when you share it with them and they begin to believe it.

_____

_____

_____

_____

_____

_____

_____

_____

OPPOSITION

OVERCOME - Learn to Overcome Doubt, Shame, and Others

Scripture - There he went into a cave and spent the night. And the word of the LORD came to him: "What are you doing here, Elijah?" He replied, "I have been very zealous for the LORD God Almighty. The Israelites have rejected your covenant, torn down your altars, and put your prophets to death with the sword. I am the only one left, and now they are trying to kill me too." (1 Kings 19:9-10)

Think About It!

God asked Elijah, "Why you are here?"

Elijah explained that he is alone, and as God's representative. He is in danger of losing the battle. God knew better. God stepped in to show Elijah that God is still all powerful.

Challenge

God has all power in Elijah's life and in ours. Do you ever feel that friends and family around you are falling and that you are the only that is still trying to be faithful to God? If so, what are they struggling with? How are you surviving? How can your testimony help them? Will the tables ever turn, leaving you stranded while they are faithfully overcoming all opposition?

Sign of Hope

We must all learn to overcome the enemy that lives inside of us, and that stands in opposition against us. He lies to us and makes us believe we are alone, but whenever we think we're alone that is a sign that God has us all alone to work on us, and if God is working on us, then remember He is working on others too. We are all in this together on the journey as a family in Christ. God help someone else if they need it. Go seek their help if you need it. Remember that you are never alone.

OVERCOME - Learn your role

Scripture - The LORD said "Go out and stand on the mountain in the presence of the LORD, for the LORD is about to pass by." Then a great and powerful wind tore the mountains apart and shattered the rocks before the LORD, but the LORD was not in the wind. After the wind there was an earthquake, but the LORD was not in the earthquake. After the earthquake came a fire, but the LORD was not in the fire. And after the fire came a gentle whisper. (1 Kings 19:11-12)

Think About It!

As you seek God and serve God, you have several important lessons to learn. You must learn about your God. You must get to know your God. Then learn your role in God. Learn the requirements of your role in God.

Though Elijah had been serving the Lord, he had to continue learning who his God really was. When God showed up this time, God wasn't in the wind. God wasn't in the earthquake, nor was God in the fire. God was in the whisper. Elijah had to learn how to discern God. He had to learn to find God in the midst of the chaos. He had to learn to hear the whisper of God. A servant must learn his / her role. A servant is a listener.

Challenge

God, do likewise. Learn how to listen. But first, how does communicate with you today?

Sign of Hope

Keep learning your leader (God) and keep learning your role as you serve your leader (God). You will know Him!

Join the Team

Scripture - When Elijah heard it, he pulled his cloak over his face and went out and stood at the mouth of the cave. Then a voice said to him, "What are you doing here, Elijah?" He replied, "I have been very zealous for the LORD God Almighty. The Israelites have rejected your covenant, torn down your altars, and put your prophets to death with the sword. I am the only one left, and now they are trying to kill me too." (1 Kings 19:13-14)

Think About It!

He came for rest, strength and to get help with his fear.
He came to get faith and hope.
God had other plans.

Elijah overcame the foot soldiers.

Now he must learn to overthrow powers and authorities.

Elijah won't do it alone. It will take a team!

Challenge

You are not the only faithful leader.
Come out of yourself and join the team!
There is a spiritual war at hand, and God is galvanizing forces for good against evil. In the end, we win. Will you join the team? What is holding you back? What is it about the team that is stopping you from joining in fully? Discuss it, then decide that you will overcome it. Nothing will stop you!

Sign of Hope

Your invitation is just a sign that there is something greater waiting at hand.

OVERCOME Effectively (Memory Verse & Action Plan)

Assurance of Prayer Memory Verse
Until now you have not asked for anything in my name. Ask and you
will receive, and your joy will be complete." John 16:24

What is the greatest gift of God?
It can be said that the greatest gift of God is His creation, where God created us
and gave us the opportunity to live. If that is not the greatest gift, then we can
agree that it is the first of God's great gifts.

Later, God sent His one and only son to atone for our sins by dying on the
cross. God raised Him from the grave and returned to heaven where He
intercedes for us through prayer. Now, if Jesus prays for us in heaven, then we
should be praying for ourselves here on earth.

Prayer is a spiritual gift that is essential for our lives. Through prayer, we are
seeking God and His direction for our lives.

Praying also helps keep us out of trouble. Jesus told us to pray, "Watch and pray
so that you will not fall into temptation." (Matthew 26:41)

**Read John 16:24 and discuss some other reasons we should pray. What
are some of the things you ask for in prayer?**

_____

_____

_____

God is ready and willing to help us when we are happy, sad, sick
or even when we're in trouble. God will give us wisdom, strength and
understanding if we only ask Him. In fact God will give us many good
things if we ask for them in accordance to His Will.

Week 12 – Day 5

God answers our prayers in many ways that we can understand. God gives us dreams, and visions. He responds through signs and wonders. His Holy Spirit moves and communicates with us audibly, and through God's Word, the Holy Bible.

Perhaps the best use of prayer is that it helps us grow in our relationship with God. Trust me, when we pray, God will answer us and God's responses will definitely help us grow. We are God's followers and servants, but as we talk to God in prayer each day, the bonding that takes place, the spiritual connection will become so much stronger and the way we feel about each other will become so much more real, that our relationship will become like a son and father, like a friend and friends. Jesus promised that He and His father will become one with us.

Read Jeremiah 29:13 and discuss the true reward of praying

_____

_____

_____

_____

_____

_____

Remember to pray earnestly, and with all of our heart!

ACTION PLAN

Review this chapter's lessons and list your OVERCOME Goals.
These are your next steps to help you BECOME

Here are some examples:

- Face my past
- Admit my wrongs
- Accept my mistakes and failures
- Recognize and admit that I face obstacles today
- We are all people with problems. We have our own fears.
- Admit my character proclivities (if I am timid and afraid or overconfident and overzealous)
- Accept my limitations in Christ (e.g. My lack of faith in God)
- Spend time each day looking at the known challenges ahead and pray for strength to conquer them

_____

_____

_____

_____

_____

_____

_____

_____

OVERCOME ACKNOWLEDGMENT

Read and sign your personal 'Agreement to become"
Ask your Discipleship Leader to sign and agree

I acknowledge that I am an overcomer. I will face tremendous opposition from family, friends, strangers, and onlookers. Some are believers, leaders, followers, and dome peers.

I will even find opposition within myself, as I may struggle with feelings of fear, doubt, shame, and regret. Despite these challenges, I am more than a conqueror. I will overcome them all and become like Jesus Christ!

_____

Disciple

I accept the responsibility to hold this disciple accountable by making sure he/she walks in humble submission and service to the Lord.

_____

Discipleship Leader

Introduction to TRANSFORM

The next phase of discipleship requires that we must all be transformed. Jesus brought his closest friends up the mountain to share a special experience with him. Jesus was transfigured before their eyes. He engaged Elijah and Moses in conversation. The divine nature of Jesus was revealed. The power of Jesus was revealed. The eternal was revealed to flesh. The transcendence of God returned to the past, summoned the prophets and returned to the present, and joined them in a private discussion. It is unique that Jesus' coming was preceded by the modern Elijah. Jesus' arrival to shepherd the people made him a modern Moses. Jesus brought the two together. It was the arrival of the King, the pivotal moment for the Israelites to be transformed into believers, finally. In this moment, Peter, James, and John witnessed the transfiguration of Jesus. Jesus allowed Peter, James and John to experience the intimacy of that experience. Jesus taught them that access to divine miracles required the vehicles of prayer and fasting. Divine faith was nourished with prayer. Focus on God and sensitivity to God's presence is strengthened by fasting. It is time to develop true spiritual power. It is offered to the transformed vessel. It is revealed in your treatment of others, your willingness to serve others. Your heart is a stewing pot of transformation.

Key lessons and events in Chapters 9-10, include:

o   Disciples were transformed through transfiguration (9:2-13)
o   Disciples were transformed through prayer & fasting (9:14-29)
o   Disciples were transformed through serving others (9:35-50)
o   Teaching to transform the heart (e.g. through marriage, children, money, and positions) (Ch. 10)

Week 13 – Day 2
Read Disciples were transformed through transfiguration (9:2-13)

Week 13 – Day 3
Read Disciples were transformed through prayer & fasting (9:14-29)

Week 13 – Day 4
Read Disciples were transformed through serving others (9:35-50)

Week 13 – Day 5
Read Teaching to transform the heart (e.g. through marriage, children, money, and positions) (Ch. 10)

Where are you being TRANSFORMED?

Read the story about the transfiguration.

After six days Jesus took Peter, James and John with him and led them up a high mountain, where they were all alone. There he was transfigured before them. ³ His clothes became dazzling white, whiter than anyone in the world could bleach them. ⁴ And there appeared before them Elijah and Moses, who were talking with Jesus.

⁵ Peter said to Jesus, "Rabbi, it is good for us to be here. Let us put up three shelters—one for you, one for Moses and one for Elijah." ⁶ (He did not know what to say, they were so frightened.)

⁷ Then a cloud appeared and covered them, and a voice came from the cloud: "This is my Son, whom I love. Listen to him!" ⁸ Suddenly, when they looked around, they no longer saw anyone with them except Jesus.

⁹ As they were coming down the mountain, Jesus gave them orders not to tell anyone what they had seen until the Son of Man had risen from the dead. ¹⁰ They kept the matter to themselves, discussing what "rising from the dead" meant.¹¹ And they asked him, "Why do the teachers of the law say that Elijah must come first?" ¹² Jesus replied, "To be sure, Elijah does come first, and restores all things. Why then is it written that the Son of Man must suffer much and be rejected? ¹³ But I tell you, Elijah has come, and they have done to him everything they wished, just as it is written about him." (Mark 9:2-13)

Jesus was transfigured but the disciples were transformed by the experience. God used symbols in this moment of transfiguration to affirm His son.

- Read Daniel 7:9 and note the similarity of how God made Jesus' clothes turn white.

- Read Malachi 4:5-6 and note the similarity of how God planned to send Elijah and Moses before Jesus to pave the way.

- Read Exodus 13:21 and note the similarity of how God used the cloud to guide the Hebrew people on their way

- Read Matthew 3:17 and note the similarity of how God spoke similar words at Jesus' baptism, saying "This is my Son, whom I love"

God turned Jesus' clothes white. It appears that His glory radiated through His being, causing His clothes to glow.

Do you get the sense that God was creating a special moment here?

_____

_____

God sent Moses and Elijah to speak with Jesus. The disciples were familiar with who Moses and Elijah were. It was as though God wanted the representatives of the law (Moses) and the representative of the prophets (Elijah) to meet with the representative of Grace (Jesus). God was moving in a new direction. God was transforming the disciples' perspective, of what God wanted Jesus to do and who He would be for the Jewish people. If they followed the Law of Moses and honored the prophets who advocated for a return to God and His law, then the disciples should have made the connection between the law, the prophets and Jesus who would perfectly obey the teachings of the law and the prophets.

Read about Jesus' teaching on the law and the prophets in Matthew 5:17-20.

Jesus did not come to nullify the requirements and teachings of the law. Instead, Jesus came to embody the principles of the law. Jesus would perfectly obey the law. He lived in a daily relationship with God, praying and listening to God, and obeying His commands.

When the disciples saw Jesus talking to Moses and Elijah, God spoke from the cloud and said, "This is my Son, whom I love. Listen to him!"

Why do you believe that God wanted to give Jesus a private affirmation again?

_____

_____

How would you have felt if you were there with Peter, James, and John watching this take place?

_____

_____

Are you spending quite time with God in prayer, in worship, listening and taking direction? Share how God is transforming you.

_____

_____

_____

_____

TRANSFORMED through prayer & fasting

Read the Bible Story about the power of fasting and prayer

[17] A man in the crowd answered, "Teacher, I brought you my son, who is possessed by a spirit that has robbed him of speech. [18] Whenever it seizes him, it throws him to the ground. He foams at the mouth, gnashes his teeth and becomes rigid. I asked your disciples to drive out the spirit, but they could not." [19] "You unbelieving generation," Jesus replied, "How long shall I stay with you? How long shall I put up with you? Bring the boy to me." [20] So they brought him. When the spirit saw Jesus, it immediately threw the boy into a convulsion. He fell to the ground and rolled around, foaming at the mouth.

[21] Jesus asked the boy's father, "How long has he been like this?" "From childhood," he answered. [22] "It has often thrown him into fire or water to kill him. But if you can do anything, take pity on us and help us." [23] "'If you can'?" said Jesus. "Everything is possible for one who believes." [24] Immediately the boy's father exclaimed, "I do believe; help me overcome my unbelief!" [25] When Jesus saw that a crowd was running to the scene, he rebuked the impure spirit. "You deaf and mute spirit," he said, "I command you, come out of him and never enter him again." [26] The spirit shrieked, convulsed him violently and came out. The boy looked so much like a corpse that many said, "He's dead." [27] But Jesus took him by the hand and lifted him to his feet, and he stood up. [28] After Jesus had gone indoors, his disciples asked him privately, "Why couldn't we drive it out?" [29] He replied, "This kind can come out only by prayer." (Mark 9:17-29)

Transformation empowers you

A man brought his son to the disciples to drive out the evil spirit, but the disciples could not do it. Then Jesus rebuked the impure spirit and commanded it to "come out of him." Jesus made the spirit came out of the boy never to enter into him again.

The Disciples had not undergone the type of transformation required to have (or take) authority of spirits.

When transformation takes place you experience inward change.

Transformation is what the Holy Spirit does to your spiritual being. It is communication with God that surpasses your, physical, emotional beings to strengthen your spirit. Your spiritual connection is less physical (sensory). Your part is reverencing God in praise and worship. It involves surrendering to God in listening, willing obedience. It requires constant

Are you expecting God to transform you? If so, how?

_____

_____

_____

_____

_____

_____

95

Discuss the Transformative Power of prayer

Remember that prayer is communicating with or talking with God. The word ACTS can help you remember what to pray for.

A is for Adoration

To adore God means to love Him simply for who He is. Adoration leads to praise, where we recognize God for what He has done.

Read aloud and write down 1 Chronicles 29:11 in adoration of God.

_____

_____

_____

_____

Read aloud and write down Psalm 145:1-2 to express adoration and praise

_____

_____

_____

_____

C is for Confession

To makes a confession to God means to admit your sins to God and to ask for His forgiveness.

Read aloud and write down 1 John 1:9

_____

_____

_____

_____

T = Thanksgiving

To express thanksgiving to God means to thank God for all of the great things that He has done in your life.

Read aloud and write down Psalm 7:17 to give God thanks.

_____

_____

_____

_____

S = Supplication

To make a supplication to God means to ask God for something.

You might make requests for yourself, family or friends.

Read aloud and write down Psalm 51:10-12

_____

_____

_____

_____

_____

_____

_____

Write your own prayer based on the ACTS theme

_____

_____

_____

_____

_____

_____

_____

_____

_____

_____

_____

_____

_____

_____

Here's how transformation looks.

One day you are fully engaged with the world around you, but you are only outwardly connected. In transformation, your spirit engages God and heaven. You become outwardly engaged with your world and you are inwardly connected. You begin to change when you let the spiritual connection with God's Holy Spirit lead you. You are transformed by the spirit led life. Then you will see that a transformed disciple can change the outcomes of life. A transformed disciple has power! How strong is your connection today? How much have you been transformed already?

_____

_____

_____

Read Psalm 63:1-8 and note when David spent time with God?

_____

_____

Daniel 1:1-17 and note why Daniel fasted? How did it help him?

_____

_____

_____

_____

_____

–

TRANSFORMED through serving others

Read the Bible Story about becoming

Sitting down, Jesus called the Twelve and said, "Anyone who wants to be first must be the very last, and the servant of all."[36] He took a little child whom he placed among them. Taking the child in his arms, he said to them, [37] "Whoever welcomes one of these little children in my name welcomes me; and whoever welcomes me does not welcome me but the one who sent me." (Mark 9:35-37)

Become a servant

Jesus gives us the rule of the kingdom. It is about service.

The culture of the world is against serving others. There is a tendency among people to be first, to go first, to get yours, that is to get what you want and to ignore other's needs.

In fact, the culture says it is ok to use others, oppressing them if necessary to get what you want.

Jesus turns this thinking around to reflect the beauty of God. God is so holy and righteous. He is different from all others. He teaches them how to be successful in God's eyes. Well, He tells them how to be first (which was their own selfish goal). Jesus says that to be first, you have to put others first and put yourself last. You have to love, and serve others first.

Read Phillipians 2:1-4. How do you imitate the love and humility of Jesus?

What is the Apostle Paul asking believers to do?

_____

_____

_____

When you value others, what types of things will you show interest in (in others)?

_____

_____

_____

Read 1 Peter 4:1-11 and note that God intends believers to use their gifts to serve others. Note that in order to do this, you have to put them first.

Are you ready to live for the kingdom by serving?

_____

_____

_____

God is giving you the opportunity to break the norm. Jesus for example, told the disciples to allow the children to come to Him. When you break the norm, you are bucking the trend. You are reshaping the norm, turning the world's systems upside down. When doing this, you will be demonstrating a power that is new to you.

Read Matthew 20:20-28

Note that you don't lord your power over people to be great! List some of the ways to be great in God's kingdom.

_____

_____

_____

As a disciple of the Lord Jesus Christ, you are required to serve others to be great. In doing so, you will not only turn the world's ways upside down, you will also position yourself to be turned upside down. Yes, you will be transformed.

Read 2 Chronicles 36:17-20, about a wicked King who lorded his power over the people. God used King Nebuchadnezzar to rule over His people. What are some of the ways King Nebuchadnezzar oppressed the people.

_____

_____

_____

Read Ezra 1:1-4 and learn about a King whose service was liberating.

Note how Cyrus, King of Persia came to fulfill the prophecy of Jeremiah. Even as a heathen, king of another nation, he served God by allowing God's people to return to Jerusalem to rebuild their temple.

Read Daniel 4:24-27 where Daniel interpreted the dream for the wicked King Nebuchadnezzar. Daniel recommended that King Nebuchadnezzar acknowledge something. What was it?

_____

_____

Daniel also told King Nebuchadnezzar that he had to do right by how he treated people. What was that?

_____

_____

Then read Daniel 4:28-33, and learn how Nebuchadnezzar fell from grace.

What could he have done to secure himself from God's wrath? How did he differ from the more gracious King Cyprus?

_____

_____

Read the Bible Story

"Teacher," said John, "we saw someone driving out demons in your name and we told him to stop, because he was not one of us."³⁹ "Do not stop him," Jesus said. "For no one who does a miracle in my name can in the next moment say anything bad about me, ⁴⁰ for whoever is not against us is for us. ⁴¹ Truly I tell you, anyone who gives you a cup of water in my name because you belong to the Messiah will certainly not lose their reward. (Mark 9:38-41)

Servants want to see the job get done!

It doesn't matter who does it or they're different or doing it differently from us than us

_____

_____

_____

TRANSFORMED through family vows

Read the Bible Story

Jesus then left that place and went into the region of Judea and across the Jordan. Again crowds of people came to him, and as was his custom, he taught them. ²Some Pharisees came and tested him by asking, "Is it lawful for a man to divorce his wife?" ³ "What did Moses command you?" he replied. ⁴They said, "Moses permitted a man to write a certificate of divorce and send her away." ⁵ "It was because your hearts were hard that Moses wrote you this law," Jesus replied. ⁶ "But at the beginning of creation God 'made them male and female.'[a] ⁷ 'For this reason a man will leave his father and mother and be united to his wife,[b] ⁸ and the two will become one flesh.'[c] So they are no longer two, but one flesh. ⁹Therefore what God has joined together, let no one separate." (Mark 9:1-12)

Discuss the transformation of heart required to sustain marriage and family relationships

Our family relationships say a lot about us. How we manage our intimate relationships (e.g. marriages) tells us about the state of our heart.

Making the commitment to marriage (for example) transforms you. It requires you to die to your own selfish interests and desires. Are you willing to deny yourself? Our self-denial and ultimate transformation is required to manage long term, life giving relationships with others. Marriage is a good example of it because it is a union that connects us at a soul level. It allows God to connect to us at a deep level where He is able to mend and mold us into the likeness of Jesus Christ.

Are you willing to stay committed? We are taught that in marriage that divorce is not an option. You will have to change in order to survive the demands of the relationship. Here's what will change: how you think, what you believe, what you want, what you do, how you think and feel about the other person

Are you willing to endure the long journey of discipleship? Sometimes suffering, with some rewards from God? What are some of the things that will change in you?

Read the Bible Story

¹³ People were bringing little children to Jesus for him to place his hands on them, but the disciples rebuked them. ¹⁴ When Jesus saw this, he was indignant. He said to them, "Let the little children come to me, and do not hinder them, for the kingdom of God belongs to such as these. ¹⁵ Truly I tell you, anyone who will not receive the kingdom of God like a little child will never enter it." ¹⁶ And he took the children in his arms, placed his hands on them and blessed them. (Mark 10:13-16)

Discuss the transformation of heart required to welcome others to Jesus Christ.

On the surface, this story teaches us that even little children should be welcomed. It requires disciples to understand that we all have ownership in the kingdom.

On a deeper level, it teaches that we all must come to Christ in a child-like way, with an open heart, open arms. In fact, when we welcome Jesus Christ and His kingdom into our hearts, we begin our journey as spiritual infants, children, growing up into mature adults.

The Apostle Paul wrote to the Church into Galatia, he said that what he felt for them were like the pains a woman feels in childbirth. The Apostle Paul was watching, ministering and praying until "Christ is formed in you." It is God's intent that we continue to grow.

Making the commitment to welcome others transforms you. Being open to transformation will cost you your old ways of thinking. The way you treat others will change. To inherit eternal life, you have to give your all!

107

TRANSFORMED by confession

Read the Bible Story

As Jesus started on his way, a man ran up to him and fell on his knees before him. "Good teacher," he asked, "what must I do to inherit eternal life?" [18] "Why do you call me good?" Jesus answered. "No one is good—except God alone. [19] You know the commandments: 'You shall not murder, you shall not commit adultery, you shall not steal, you shall not give false testimony, you shall not defraud, honor your father and mother.'" [20] "Teacher," he declared, "all these I have kept since I was a boy." [21] Jesus looked at him and loved him. "One thing you lack," he said. "Go, sell everything you have and give to the poor, and you will have treasure in heaven. Then come, follow me." [22] At this the man's face fell. He went away sad, because he had great wealth. [23] Jesus looked around and said to his disciples, "How hard it is for the rich to enter the kingdom of God!" [4] The disciples were amazed at his words. But Jesus said again, "Children, how hard it is to enter the kingdom of God! [25] It is easier for a camel to go through the eye of a needle than for someone who is rich to enter the kingdom of God." [26] The disciples were even more amazed, and said to each other, "Who then can be saved?" [27] Jesus looked at them and said, "With man this is impossible, but not with God; all things are possible with God." (Mark 10:17-27)

This story addresses the biggest question of all. How do I inherit eternal life? How do I get to heaven? When the man addresses Jesus as good teacher, Jesus explains that no one is good except God alone. So, being good does not get you into heaven.

Then Jesus tells the man to know (and obey) the commandments. The young man explains that he has kept them since he was a boy. Again, your ability to follow the law was no guarantee to get you into heaven.

In fact, what God would wanted everyone to know is that it was impossible to perfectly keep all of the commandments of the law.

Read Psalm 14:2-3 and note the state of the heart of man.

_____

_____

_____

That's why Jesus came, to offer us grace. Since we cannot fully keep the law. We should be honest with ourselves and admit this to God. I am a sinner and do not deserve eternal life.

Read Romans 3:20. Identify what the Old Testament Law promises and what it doesn't.

_____

_____

_____

The truth is, we all have sinned, and have to pay the penalty for sin; therefore we should accept God's act of grace. We do this by following Jesus, receiving the offer of salvation when he died for us on the cross. Then we can enjoy His offer of Lordship, where we will follow Him, reproduce (do) the works that He does, overcome all opposition in our paths and Transform into the likeness of Jesus Christ, and Master the journey of discipleship. It is in Him, that we inherit eternal life.

Then Jesus told him to sell everything he has, give it to the poor to get treasure in heaven. Then the man can begin to follow Jesus and begin his ascent to heaven. The man knew he would not want to part with his riches; therefore he could not make room in his heart for the kingdom of God and its promise of heaven.

In essence, when asked "what must I do to inherit eternal life", Jesus told the rich young ruler to give up all that he had and surrender to Jesus. Jesus was welcoming the young man to join Him on the road to salvation.

Romans 3:10, 23 and list the problem(s) that all people have in common

_____

_____

_____

Read Romans 6:23 and consider the consequences of our sin.

What is the penalty for sin? What kind of death is it?
Do we literally die on the spot when we sin? Is it a physical death or spiritual? What is God offering you instead?

_____

_____

_____

_____

_____

_____

For the wages of sin is death, but the gift of God is eternal life in Christ Jesus our Lord. Wages are payments required for doing something. We make payments to others for using their services. God established the rule in His created world, that because we all sin, the wages we have to pay for sin is death. It is a spiritual death where we are spiritually separated from God.

God, however, offered us a free gift, to use for our payment. It allows us to enjoy another gift from God. It allows us to live forever with Jesus. If we accept the gift, we don't have to pay the penalty of living in spiritual death! Instead we get eternal life (forever).

111

Read Romans 5:8 and note why this gift was offered.

_____

Read Romans 10:9, 13. How do you secure God's gift of eternal life?

_____

_____

_____

Inheriting Eternal life requires some reflection.

Can you identify what your heart has and cherishes most?

_____

_____

_____

Now weigh it against God. What does God provide to those who cherish Him?

_____

_____

_____

Now choose God!

Read 1 Kings 18:16-20.

Why were the people trapped between serving God and serving a false god (idol)?

_____

_____

Now read 1 Kings 38-39 and see who they chose!

_____

_____

Let's take a look at how the theme transform unfolds in the life of the prophet Elijah. Let's look at what it means to transform.

(Lead while Preparing Others)
You will learn to serve someone else before you learn to lead others!

TRANSFORM - Prepare a successor

Scripture

The LORD said to him, "Go back the way you came, and go to the Desert of Damascus. When you get there, anoint Hazael king over Aram. Also, anoint Jehu son of Nimshi king over Israel, and anoint Elisha son of Shaphat from Abel Meholah to succeed you as prophet. (1 Kings 19:15-16)

Think About It!

The farther you go, the farther you must also return. In the kingdom of God, you are not on a journey alone. You are on a journey with others. Though you may surpass others sometimes, and go on into unknown territory, to conquer new lands, and do great things, you may have to prepare others to manage it, succeed you and someday own it. Elijah traveled a long way, then he went back the way he came to prepare successors. He anointed the next King of Aram, the next king over Israel and his replacement, the next major prophet. By obeying God and going back, Elijah soon realized that he was not as alone as he thought.

Challenge

Have you ever had an assignment that you believed only you could do? God will show you that He has been preparing others all along to carry His ministry forth, the same way He has equipped you. Do you have someone that you can bring along to walk alongside you? Who can you pour into? Trust God as He transforms you, He will use you to transform others.

Sign of Hope

You know that God is changing you when you are courageous enough to strive farther. The new season you are in demands that you press forward and break new ground. Remember to only look back to lead others.

TRANSFORM - Prepare a roadmap

Scripture

Jehu will put to death any who escape the sword of Hazael, and Elisha will put to death any who escape the sword of Jehu. Yet I reserve seven thousand in Israel—all whose knees have not bowed down to Baal and whose mouths have not kissed him." (1 Kings 19:17-18)

Think About It

God is giving you the chance to join in with Him to see do wondrous things. If you are willing to help those who will follow you, then you will see endless victories accomplished in the name of our God.

If you agree to prepare a roadmap for those who will follow you, then you will also see generation of kingdom building in the name of God. It is a beautiful thing to serve god knowing that nothing will happen to you because your work is not done and because you have others to prepare that are following you.

Challenge

Have you ever had a great season of success or victory end, only to see others arise and come into their own? How did it feel? Were you able to celebrate with them? How does it feel to know that you have helped someone prepare for their own season of ministry?

Sign of Hope

You may have to start something or clean up something.
Get ready! You may have to rebuild or launch out farther.
You know that God is not through with you yet, and that He has more for you to do, when others behind you are doing greater works of faith.
That means the work is passing from your hands to theirs. You must prepare them!

TRANSFORM - Show them the Pitfalls

Scripture

So Elijah went from there and found Elisha son of Shaphat. He was plowing with twelve yoke of oxen, and he himself was driving the twelfth pair. Elijah went up to him and threw his cloak around him. Elisha then left his oxen and ran after Elijah. "Let me kiss my father and mother goodbye," he said, "and then I will come with you." "Go back," Elijah replied. "What have I done to you?" (1 Kings 19:19-20)

Think About It!

Show them the path to success. Show them the pitfalls that they will encounter and show them how to overcome them.

Sign of Hope

Both Elijah and Elisha left a lot behind. Elijah became much more than he could have imagined. You will become if you are ready when God is ready for you.

TRANSFORM Effectively (Memory Verse & Action Plan)

Assurance of Faith Memory Verse

Now faith is confidence in what we hope for and assurance about what we do not see. And without faith it is impossible to please God, because anyone who comes to him must believe that he exists and that he rewards those who earnestly seek him. Hebrews 11:1, 6

Read the first sentence aloud and write it below

_____

_____

Read the 2nd part of the text aloud and write it below

_____

_____

Read the 3rd part of the text aloud and write it below

_____

_____

Read the 4th part of the text aloud and write it below

_____

_____

Reread the scripture again up to 7 times.

ACTION PLAN

Review this chapter's lessons and list your TRANSFORM Goals.
These are your next steps to help you BECOME

Here are some examples:

- Reflect on the highs and lows of the life you have today
- Think on what you are not handling well,
- What hurts, struggles, shortcomings, weaknesses do you have that prevent you from walking with authority
- Admit that you need to be transformed
- Dedicate time each week to experience the presence of God.
- Welcome in His Holy Spirit into your heart each day
- Commit to a day of prayer and fasting each week, month or year
- Thank God each morning and Ask for spiritual power before your feet hit the floor each day

_____

_____

_____

_____

_____

_____

_____

Read and sign your personal 'Agreement to become"

Ask your Discipleship Leader to sign and agree

I acknowledge and agree that I will be transformed. I will be a pure and holy vessel used by God to demonstrate true spiritual power. I will love others and serve them the way Jesus does. I will commit to transformation, whatever the cost!

_____

Disciple

I accept the responsibility to hold this disciple accountable by making sure he/she walks in humble submission and service to the Lord.

_____

Discipleship Leader

Recap Phases 3 & 4 - Overcoming & Transforming

Moses, the overcomer and transformer

Now let's take a look at Moses who does an excellent job of transitioning the ministry into the hands of the next leader.

Moses' Roadmap

Moses prepared a roadmap for the Hebrew children to show them the broad future which entails all the their possibilities Deuteronomy 6:1-3 says "These are the commands, decrees and laws the LORD your God directed me to teach you to observe in the land that you are crossing the Jordan to possess, ² so that you, your children and their children after them may fear the LORD your God as long as you live by keeping all his decrees and commands that I give you, and so that you may enjoy long life. ³ Hear, Israel, and be careful to obey so that it may go well with you and that you may increase greatly in a land flowing with milk and honey, just as the LORD, the God of your ancestors, promised you." Moses laid out the truth for Israel before they settled into their promised land.

Moses showed the pitfalls

Moses also showed them the pitfalls that they'd face and how to overcome them. Deuteronomy 6:10-12 says, "When the LORD your God brings you into the land he swore to your fathers, to Abraham, Isaac and Jacob, to give you—a land with large, flourishing cities you did not build, ¹¹ houses filled with all kinds of good things you did not provide, wells

121

you did not dig, and vineyards and olive groves you did not plant—then when you eat and are satisfied, [12] be careful that you do not forget the LORD, who brought you out of Egypt, out of the land of slavery." Moses taught them not to forget God.

Moses documented the unwritten

Lastly, Moses was able to take the initiative to do things that aren't written. There are things you'll have to venture out and discover for yourself . There are goals you will have to dig up the courage to explore.

In Deuteronomy 6:13-25, Moses writes, "Fear the LORD your God, serve him only and take your oaths in his name. Do not follow other gods, the gods of the peoples around you; for the LORD your God, who is among you, is a jealous God and his anger will burn against you, and he will destroy you from the face of the land. Do not put the LORD your God to the test as you did at Massah. Be sure to keep the commands of the LORD your God and the stipulations and decrees he has given you. Do what is right and good in the LORD's sight, so that it may go well with you and you may go in and take over the good land the LORD promised on oath to your ancestors, thrusting out all your enemies before you, as the LORD said.

In the future, when your son asks you, "What is the meaning of the stipulations, decrees and laws the LORD our God has commanded you?" tell him: "We were slaves of Pharaoh in Egypt, but the LORD brought us out of Egypt with a mighty hand. Before our eyes the LORD sent signs and wonders—great and terrible—on Egypt and Pharaoh and his whole household. But he brought us out from there to bring us in and give us the land he promised on oath to our ancestors. The LORD commanded us to obey all these decrees and to fear the LORD our God, so that we might always prosper and be kept alive, as is the case today. And if we are careful to obey all this law before the LORD our God, as he has commanded us that will be our righteousness."

Phase 5 – Introduction to MASTER

Jesus and company approached Jerusalem for His triumphant entry. To its dismay, Jesus cursed a fig tree for appearing to produce fruit but failing to do so. He also rebuked the Pharisees for public displays of public piety with no inward transformation. Jesus clearly called for integrity where inward motives equaled external presentations. Jesus also pointed to future events and His second coming, as He planned to exit His first coming. Jesus purposed to please the father with loving obedience. This was displayed as He bore the cross of Calvary. Jesus' passion included suffering but it ended with conquering. The Lord Jesus suffered, bled and died for our sins. Later, Jesus' resurrection and reappearances showed God's power over death. Jesus showed us how to master what it means to be a disciple.

Key lessons and events in Mark Chapters 11-16 include:

o   MASTER Triumphant Entries (Ch. 11)

o   MASTER public performance with inward piety (Ch. 12)

o   MASTER seeing signs and wonders (Ch. 13)

o   MASTER Preparation, last supper; (14:1-26)

o   MASTER Commitments & Denials (14:66-72)

o   MASTER mockery, persecution and crucifixion (15:1-32)

o   MASTER death, and resurrection (15:33-16:8)

o   MASTER reappearances and testimonials (16:9-16:20)

MASTER the triumphs & tragedies

Read the Bible Story

As they approached Jerusalem and came to Bethphage and Bethany at the Mount of Olives, Jesus sent two of his disciples, ² saying to them, "Go to the village ahead of you, and just as you enter it, you will find a colt tied there, which no one has ever ridden. Untie it and bring it here. ³ If anyone asks you, 'Why are you doing this?' say, 'The Lord needs it and will send it back here shortly.'"

⁴ They went and found a colt outside in the street, tied at a doorway. As they untied it, ⁵ some people standing there asked, "What are you doing, untying that colt?" ⁶ They answered as Jesus had told them to, and the people let them go. ⁷ When they brought the colt to Jesus and threw their cloaks over it, he sat on it. ⁸ Many people spread their cloaks on the road, while others spread branches they had cut in the fields. ⁹ Those who went ahead and those who followed shouted, "Hosanna!" "Blessed is he who comes in the name of the Lord!" ¹⁰ "Blessed is the coming kingdom of our father David!" "Hosanna in the highest heaven!" (Mark 11:1-20)

Disciples must learn to balance the celebrations and the suffering

The story of the Triumphant Entry is a representation of God's triumph over evil. In one respect, it is meant to remind us that God has overcome our enemy. It is also meant to strengthen our hearts. For, if Jesus conquered evil, then so will we. In this pivotal moment, Jesus gives Jerusalem the opportunity to recognize His Lordship.

If the disciples understood what was happening, it would have been both a time of journey and at the same time, it was a time of celebration. For the king of glory was closer to the moment of victory.

For Jesus, it was beginning of the end. He was nearing the moment of crucifixion and He had to go through it. This act would bring death to His human life but it would bring eternal salvation for all souls who would believe!

For the disciples, it is a reminder that they will have to master the journey of discipleship. There is such a duality to serving God. At times, there is a hard task that we have to go and do that brings a free gift to someone else who will not have to do anything to get it. Approaching such a moment, the disciples will learn to enjoy the celebration along with the suffering. They will have to accept the recognition, though they aren't deserving.

Read Exodus 2:11-15.

Recall how quickly we go from loved and respected to hated. How did the opinion on Moses change?

_____

_____

_____

Disciples must master the dynamic shifts in the atmosphere. On the surface, it appears one way, but the spirit world will reveal something altogether different.

Disciples must learn to handle the celebration knowing that the crucifixion is ahead. Some of them will receive you and celebrate you but not your message.

Read the Bible Story about Jesus' teaching on public fraud vs. inward piety

Jesus sat down opposite the place where the offerings were put and watched the crowd putting their money into the temple treasury. Many rich people threw in large amounts. [42] But a poor widow came and put in two very small copper coins, worth only a few cents. [43] Calling his disciples to him, Jesus said, "Truly I tell you, this poor widow has put more into the treasury than all the others. [44] They all gave out of their wealth; but she, out of her poverty, put in everything—all she had to live on." (Ch. 12:41-44)

This is a lesson on trusting God with all you've got!

The disciples would have to learn to give up everything and live on what Jesus provides. That is tough to do. For the disciple, it is not a one-time act of sacrifice. It is an ongoing shedding of what you have and a taking on of what the Lord wants you to have. What are you lacking in life? Are your finances, friendships, lacking? Maybe God is requiring you to "live on Him" and what He provides.

_____

_____

_____

(Day 31) MASTER the Commitment

Read the Bible Story

[17] When evening came, Jesus arrived with the Twelve. [18] While they were reclining at the table eating, he said, "Truly I tell you, one of you will betray me—one who is eating with me." [19] They were saddened, and one by one they said to him, "Surely you don't mean me?"

[20] "It is one of the Twelve," he replied, "one who dips bread into the bowl with me. [21] The Son of Man will go just as it is written about him. But woe to that man who betrays the Son of Man! It would be better for him if he had not been born."

[22] While they were eating, Jesus took bread, and when he had given thanks, he broke it and gave it to his disciples, saying, "Take it; this is my body." [23] Then he took a cup, and when he had given thanks, he gave it to them, and they all drank from it. [24] "This is my blood of the covenant, which is poured out for many," he said to them. [25] "Truly I tell you, I will not drink again from the fruit of the vine until that day when I drink it new in the kingdom of God." [26] When they had sung a hymn, they went out to the Mount of Olives. (Mark 14:17-26)

Jesus met with his twelve disciples to celebrate Passover, as it was done every year. Jesus knew that His time had come. He knew that His own body would be crucified and His blood would be poured out for us all.

Jesus was introducing the Lord's Supper to His faithful followers and one who would betray Him. Judas was about to bring Jesus' accusers to Him in the garden where He would be arrested. He believed that He knew better than Jesus. He wanted Jesus to respond to His accusers with physical violence, which would lead to His ascension to the throne, where He would show the world that He is the King of the Jews.

Even when we think we know better than Jesus and choose to follow our own will versus God's will, God still accepts us. He still welcomes us into His presence and allows us to continue following Him. Here Jesus is teaching His disciples to take the Lord's Supper (communion), to help them remember that Jesus sacrificed Himself for us and one of His disciples was so opposed to Jesus' mission that He was trying to put an end to it. Jesus was mastering His commitment to the father. Judas was failing in his commitment as a disciple.

Read about the Hebrews Boys' commitment in Daniel 3:15-18.

Discuss what it means to remain faithful to God.

_____

_____

_____

MASTER Persecution

Read the Bible Story

It was nine in the morning when they crucified him. ²⁶ The written notice of the charge against him read: THE KING OF THE JEWS.

They crucified two rebels with him, one on his right and one on his left. Those who passed by hurled insults at him, shaking their heads and saying, "So! You who are going to destroy the temple and build it in three days, come down from the cross and save yourself!" In the same way the chief priests and the teachers of the law mocked him among themselves. "He saved others," they said, "but he can't save himself! Let this Messiah, this king of Israel, come down now from the cross that we may see and believe." Those crucified with him also heaped insults on him.

At noon, darkness came over the whole land until three in the afternoon. ³⁴ And at three in the afternoon Jesus cried out in a loud voice, *"Eloi, Eloi, lema sabachthani?"* (which means "My God, my God, why have you forsaken me?").

³⁵ When some of those standing near heard this, they said, "Listen, he's calling Elijah." ³⁶ Someone ran, filled a sponge with wine vinegar, put it on a staff, and offered it to Jesus to drink. "Now leave him alone. Let's see if Elijah comes to take him down," he said.

³⁷ With a loud cry, Jesus breathed his last. ³⁸ The curtain of the temple was torn in two from top to bottom. ³⁹ And when the centurion, who stood there in front of Jesus, saw how he died, he said, "Surely this man was the Son of God!" (Mark 15:25-39)

Jesus was wrongfully accused and persecuted. He was crucified between two thieves who broke the law and deserved to die.

How did people treat Jesus while he was on the cross?

_____

_____

_____

Red Isaiah 53:1-9 and discuss what Jesus suffered for us

_____

_____

_____

In His death there is life for us.

Read Isaiah 55:6-7. In His invitation, what is the Lord requiring?

_____

_____

_____

As a disciple, mastering persecution, you will become the suffering servant (like Jesus). There are times you will be persecuted crucified, and it will feel like death for you too. To master this season, cling to His word. Lean on His promises.

Read Isaiah 55:10-12. What does God promise to you?

_____

_____

_____

Know that God will continually bring you out, as you grow and become like Jesus

Read Phillipians 3:10. What should you strive for when your whole world is collapsing in on you?

_____

_____

_____

Keep in mind that as you go through, you will be rewarded for following Jesus' example. On the Day of Judgment, you will have confidence if in this world, you have become like Christ Jesus (1 John 4:17)

How to MASTER the Journey (Lessons from Elijah)

Let's take a look at how the theme MASTER unfolds in the life of the prophet Elijah. Let's look at what it means to MASTER

MASTER – Learn upwards

Learn from someone who is there

Scripture

Moses said to the LORD, [16] "May the LORD, the God who gives breath to all living things, appoint someone over this community [17] to go out and come in before them, one who will lead them out and bring them in, so the LORD's people will not be like sheep without a shepherd." So the LORD said to Moses, "Take Joshua son of Nun, a man in whom is the spirit of leadership and lay your hand on him. (Numbers 27:15-18)

Think About It!

Every good thing must end. Everyone has their season of glory. Every time God speaks, something happens, something changes. God spoke and declared that Moses' time was up. Moses had to prepare his successor, Joshua and show him the way. Joshua had to lean upwards into his successor to see his revelation, catch his vision, and begin learning what it took.

Challenge

Are you covered by mentorship? Do you have someone who watches out for you? Who have you given permission to show you where you're going wrong or have gone wrong? Ask God for divine intervention from a man or woman who is anointed to see beyond your next step!

Sign of Hope

It's time to lean into your leader for a glimpse of what they see and do. Go see what's waiting for you. It's waiting on you.

MASTER – Get prepared

Scripture

After the death of Moses the servant of the LORD, the LORD said to Joshua son of Nun, Moses' aide: [2] "Moses my servant is dead. Now then, you and all these people, get ready to cross the Jordan River into the land I am about to give to them—to the Israelites. [3] I will give you every place where you set your foot, as I promised Moses. [4] Your territory will extend from the desert to Lebanon, and from the great river, the Euphrates—all the Hittite country—to the Mediterranean Sea in the west. [5] No one will be able to stand against you all the days of your life. As I was with Moses, so I will be with you; I will never leave you nor forsake you. [6] Be strong and courageous, because you will lead these people to inherit the land I swore to their ancestors to give them. (Joshua 1:1-5)

Think About It!

You've got to get prepared. God is taking you where others could not go. He's planned something for you. Moses was great, but Joshua would be great too. Moses brought the people out, but Joshua would take them higher. God has new, unbroken ground waiting for you.

Challenge

Why do you like old ground? Are you comfortable there? Are you ready to go farther, and do more for God? Are you content with whoever and however you are? Do you sense that there is a new you waiting to break out? There is new ground within you. Give yourself tgo God and ask God to change you!

Sign of Hope

Be strong and courageous so you can go where God is taking you!

MASTER Effectively (Memory Verse & Action Plan)

Assurance of Promises - Memory Verse
For God so loved the world that he gave his one and only Son, that
whoever believes in him shall not perish but have eternal life.
John 3:16

Read the first sentence aloud and write it below

_____

_____

_____

Read the 2nd part of the text aloud and write it below

_____

_____

_____

Reread the scripture again up to 7 times.

ACTION PLAN

Review this chapter's lessons and list your MASTER Goals.
These are your next steps to help you BECOME

Here are some examples:

- Recall the highlights and low moments in life and accept them both as God's will
- Look at the areas of life where I am supposed to produce fruit. Call out the fruit and make a daily reminder
- Commit to a daily walk of loving obedience to God, loving self-care of myself and loving kindness toward others
- Monitor your actions each day to see which problems, relationships, and challenges trip you up. Seek God for help mastering them

_____

_____

_____

_____

_____

_____

_____

_____

Acknowledgment

Read and sign your personal 'Agreement to become"

Ask your Discipleship Leader to sign and agree

I acknowledge that I will develop integrity by testing my inward motives. I will endure suffering knowing that if I am faithful, I will master my own spiritual development. Through it I will be conquering. I will Feed my spirit constantly with spirit filled praying and scriptural reading. I will Fuel my inward transformation to Prepare for the second coming of Jesus Christ. I will Master my journey!

_____

Disciple

I accept the responsibility to hold this disciple accountable by making sure he/she walks in humble submission and service to the Lord.

_____

Discipleship Leader

When you plateau, get active where you are!

Know your Location!

You will have to be where you are until God moves you. That means you must ignore the hurt, pain, resentment, frustration, bitterness associated with where you are life, in your system, in your process. Learn to be where you are. Be patient and endure the hard work of your current assignment. Master it. Dig into the details associated with it. Prepare those behind you while getting prepared for what is before. That is dually hard work. Find contentment in where you are. You have a substantial, good role that you play. You won't see it until you have prepared your predecessors and have moved on a time or two. You will have to Be a light where you are, you just might influence those above, below, those that are more / less important than you. That makes you needed. Celebrate where you are. Praise God because you are in a system.

Get the right kind of Recognition!

Recognize that you may have a small, seemingly insignificant role in a system, but the system that you are in will change. It is far better to have a small role in a good system than to have a large role in a small or bad system. The greater scope, vision, world view is better than the position, role, power. Remember David said he'd rather be a doorman in the house of the Lord than the other stuff.

Get the right kind of Success

- o Success is being able to find contentment in your assignment
- o Success is having contentment regardless of the amount of power, and authority given to you.
- o Success is measured by your ability to stop and take a breather and actually enjoy the place of rest within your assignment (when needed).
- o Success is not measured by the stuff that you got along the way

The key

It is a whole lot easier to work smarter and be content, by follow-ship, than to work very hard struggling to get to the top, with no end in sight, and no success in the present, and no benefit in the past. It only takes a little leadership and a little following to chart your course in the right direction.

The bible puts it this way, "The wisdom of the prudent is to understand his way. There is a way which seemeth right unto a man, but the end thereof are the ways of death." (Psalm 14:8a, 12 KJV)

Closing Reminder

Remember that along the journey, God will develop the leader in you. God will plant you as a seed, where you will serve Him. You may serve under someone else's authority. You may start a work for the Lord or you may succeed someone and their assignment as you carry out a mission for God. Either way, it's your assignment to seek out God's will where you are. You are not there to make your name great, to make yourself king, to be the centerpiece in others' lives. You are only there to serve God and obey. God has a plan in mind to help you become like Christ, but you've got to learn to follow first. For, the Lord of the harvest assigns us with faith based mission work, right where we are in the world.

You will learn that leadership really means doing what needs to be done and doing it in such a way that others follow. As a leader, you may have to meet the needs of others, or you may have to act on your leaders' wishes, by implementing their plans. You will learn to balance your leadership's guidance with your needs and the needs of those you serve.

In church, there is apostolic succession. In business, there is succession planning. In most organizations, there is a hierarchy, where guidance and direction begins with one person or body of authority and is shared outward. When you learn to receive that guidance and direction and implement it as necessary, you will experience true discipleship.

For true discipleship, it is essential that you learn to obey! That's the foundation for leadership. A ship's captain learns to navigate the course for a successful journey. A chef learns a recipe and makes a meal. That's your job. Find what must be done then do it. As you develop the skill of obedience you should develop the discipline of service. So, serve first! Develop humility and serve. It is essential. It will help you learn to follow and obey.

Many of us know someone providing leadership at a level that we desire. When we develop a relationship with that person, oftentimes, he or she will be able to discern where you are and where you are going. They know what you will be, what you will do, where you are going, and how well you will fare. Your responsibility will be to get to know the person, their style, their flow, what they have to offer, and what they're currently doing. Your leader has an assignment as well; learn it, then figure out what they need to have done that no one wants to do. Figure out how to help them do the worst, most painful job there is. Then do it for them in such a way that they will never have to worry about doing it or ensuring it gets done. Support them.

Support them by learning your role. In doing so, you are making or cutting out a place for yourself. This makes you a team player. So, join the team, it will help you become a great leader later.

While you're learning your role, it's a great time to start preparing your successor. Now, you have to find that person who will replace you on the assignment. Prepare that person. Prepare a roadmap for that person to succeed. Show them what's necessary to go from beginning on the assignment to mastering it. Lay out the crumbs so they can follow you out. You will have to identify the pitfalls for them. That person will have to learn to forecast their own path, which includes learning to forecast their own path, which includes leaning further in to their leader (you) to continue following you. They will continue gleaning from you to get prepared for each new level (or stop)! Someone following will learn to follow, reproduce, overcome, transform and suffer.

Part II – Get to work on your Action Plan

List all of your Action Steps and Get to Work

FOLLOW

_____

_____

_____

_____

_____

REPRODUCE

_____

_____

_____

_____

_____

_____

OVERCOME

TRANSFORM

MASTER

---

www.ingramcontent.com/pod-product-compliance
Lightning Source LLC
Chambersburg PA
CBHW031552040426
42452CB00006B/272